Try It Like This

How to Avoid the Hard Way

By

Jarrod Welsh

ISBN: 978-1-7360052-4-8

Cover design by: Melissa Welsh, Cassidy Welsh
Library of Congress Control Number: 1-9538279881
Printed in the United States of America

Contents

FOREWARD:

This book is packed with lessons I've learned that can help you bypass some pitfalls in life to avoid doing things the "hard way". The information within can transport you to a new plane of existence by giving you some tools you'll need to succeed at everything you do in life. A bold claim? Perhaps. You may already have a wonderful and fulfilling life where all your problems have vanished and it's nothing but smooth sailing for you. Or, you may be having a rough go of it and seem like everything you do results in disaster. Or you may be somewhere in between, winning some, losing some, having the proverbial "ups and downs". Regardless of your situation, this book will satisfy the needs of all three of you.

This book is not designed to make you an expert on these things, it is simply a collection of observations, lessons, and notes that I've accumulated through the years that I feel should be shared.

This book has no agenda. It's not meant to offend, although it certainly will, but bring to light issues that affect us all and possibly fix them? It will be lighthearted in some places while downright mean in others. It'll expose injustices and suggest solutions while providing encouragement and assistance in ascending above the minutia to truly be happy, regardless of what life throws at you.

This book's focus is to start dialogues and provide information on things that you might not have experienced or may have experienced but weren't sure what to do about them. For some it'll be redundant and others an eye opener – either way, here is my info for those who do want answers or would like to comment on what they read:

jarrod@tryitlikethis.net.

Chapter 1

Life Lessons

When I first joined the military, I was introduced to a thing called a continuity book. A continuity book, for those who don't know, is a binder that contains all the information regarding a certain program so, in the event that the primary person responsible for that program was gone, anyone else could pick up that book and perform the job. For instance, there was a training program that had a continuity book, and in that continuity book were checklists and regulations spelling out just how the training manager would implement, document, and report training, etc. I discuss this elsewhere in this book but I didn't learn very many life lessons as a child so it occurred to me that there should be a continuity book for life! A place to go to find out how to do any given task or information on any given

subject. Fortunately for us we have the internet and can do

just as I described but, given the fact that I joined the

military in March of 1991, the internet wouldn't really be

humming for a couple more years and not very helpful

when I came to this realization. Thankfully, it is the

juggernaut that it is so my kids don't have to endure what I

did when I was their age. Unfortunately, not all the

information you seek is readily available, it is often hidden

within lengthy articles that have laborious intros that you

must either slog through or scroll past to find the nugget of

information you seek (did you just say, "kinda like this

paragraph?" Sorry, you're right). But, hopefully, this book

can be a kind of "continuity book" for life. Let's get into it.

Overcoming Mental Barriers

I'd like to start with a person's ability to surpass

their mental limitations to achieve physical goals. I speak

to so many people who claim they can't do something

because they're too tired, or unmotivated, or simply don't believe it is possible. What I say to them is "just try". Your body can do significantly more than your mind thinks it can. Just try! Think about something else while you're doing the task/activity, your favorite song, a movie, etc. Put your mind somewhere else and just let your body take over. This was a technique I used in the military when in training or combat. Focusing on the task at hand, and trying not to get killed, was a great distraction from the pain of walking for miles, or the discomfort of being packed like sardines in the back of a helicopter or driving for hours in a cramped truck over extremely rough and bumpy terrain…at night. Focusing on other things gets you through an otherwise unbearable event. It's very simple, and can be easy, but we want to focus so much on our pain that we find it difficult to compartmentalize it. But you must look at these situations as challenges and use them to grow and eventually rise above them and be able to look at them objectively. This will allow you to assess the situation and use it to progress while not being affected emotionally.

A great way to stay motivated is to get help – heck, you can email me anytime you need some motivation – jarrod@tryitlikethis.net. I can honestly say that I wouldn't have accomplished half the things I have if there wasn't someone else there to motivate me. They didn't necessarily do anything at all except be present, but their presence was enough to keep me going because I didn't want to disappoint them, or wanted to impress them, or I couldn't let them beat me. Regardless of the reason, having someone there while you are doing these seemingly "impossible" things is very helpful, but you must decide how you want to be motivated. Do you need someone to yell at you, or coddle you, or simply be there to help you along? Do you hate when someone seems fake when they are "motivating" you? I know I do; I hate that false motivation that some try to impart. But that's just me, others need someone to get in their grill and hold them accountable.

Speaking of compartmentalization, it is an invaluable task that you need to learn in order to be successful. I talk a lot about controlling your actions in this book and compartmentalizing information is a great tool to do this. When you are exposed to information that is either good or bad, it's not always appropriate to act on that information right then. Sometimes you need to place that information in a "lock box" in your mind to either revisit when suitable or maybe not at all. This can save you from embarrassment, being fired, or just grief in general. Some say that you have to "deal" with negative feelings or they will eventually come up at an inopportune time and be a detriment to your life. I don't necessarily agree with that advice. If you can compartmentalize that information, I mean truly lock it away and not think about it, then you are free to focus on more important things. I say more important because usually this negative information isn't doing anything to help your growth and is a barricade to reaching a higher plane. Why dwell on horrible things from the past? I say rise above it and grow stronger from it. Don't allow the garbage from your past to control your present and, more importantly, your future. What's done is done and we can't change it, but we can learn from it and grow stronger.

Now, as I said, you may only need to, or be able to, compartmentalize the information for a certain amount of time. This is fine because you only need to do it until you can get to a point in your life where you can or, more importantly, want to talk about the information with a trustworthy person in a safe place. You definitely don't want the information to affect your personal or professional life. You want to control when and where you deal with that information to ensure you maintain control. But, as I said, this may be a "quick fix" until you can talk about the issue. If the information is slipping out of the brain "lock box", and it is negatively affecting your life, then you must talk about it as soon as possible. When you keep overwhelmingly troublesome information to yourself your imagination turns that piece of information into a gargantuan, and sometimes uncontrollable, problem. Getting that piece of information out into the "real world" makes it small, finite, and controllable. This controllable piece of information can now be dissected by someone else who will either provide moral support, good advice, or horrible guidance. Either way, you have now made that problem small and can safely put it back into its lock box for as long as you like. You will now be able to open the lock box at will and look at the issue as a third party instead of an active participant, allowing you to objectively evaluate the situation.

Decision Making

There is a right way and a wrong way to do things. As we grow older, we should be able to pick out the right thing over the wrong thing more often than not. We should also be honest with ourselves because we know those wrong decisions often result in adverse reactions. Some think there could be a plan laid out for us all and, good or bad, everything happens for a reason. Others think there could be a plan and we have the ability to deviate from the plan to our own detriment. Still others think our subconscious drives us and guides us to the right decision, but we sometimes deviate for our own selfish or lazy reasons. This is why the decision-making process is so important. We are constantly presented with choices and we must evaluate those choices to ensure we're making the right decision. Often the solution seems overtly apparent but still, take a few extra seconds to evaluate the other options to make sure the decision is sound. As you make this a part of your life your decision-making process will become faster and better and you'll be able to cut down your reaction time considerably. Sometimes we feel like the decision is hard but it's often our own ego or willful ignorance that stands in our way. As the issues grow in importance, so should your focus on the decision-making process but, usually the right answer presents itself pretty quickly based on your desires. The most recognizable example that comes to mind is trying to choose work or family. Obviously, the optimal answer is maximum time with your family while still providing a comfortable lifestyle. Not all of us have this luxury and must choose work over family to ensure they have what they need. This is where being selfless is key in order to create the right environment for those who rely on you. Now, some of you don't have any dependents and your decision is whether or not to work more to set yourself up for the future or to work less and have more fun right now. Both can be right depending on your goals but, if you're blowing all of your money as soon as you get it then you're not making the right decision. There are ways to have fun and still have a financial safety net for the future, it just takes discipline. So, decision making is about sifting through the chaff and focusing on what will make your life better and assist in your ascension.

My Pitch for Military Service

This next part might seem like it should be in the "Military Experience" section, but I think it's more of a life lesson. I truly believe that most, if not all people should join the military for a couple of years, at least. We hear about how young adults have exorbitant amounts of student loan debt, can't find jobs, may not have any skills or purpose, or still live with their parents. You may actually be in this situation. I believe that the military could be your ticket out. At the very least, the military will provide a place for you to stay, feed you, provide the opportunity to be healthy, and teach you several skills. At the most the military will pay for your college, allow you to see the world for free, and pay you a competitive wage. Yes, there is a chance you might die but not nearly as much as you think. Most military members don't even go to a "combat zone" let alone find themselves in "harm's way". Most military members are support personnel who perform jobs for those select few who actually go to combat. That's not to say that the other jobs are not important, they are essential to allow the warfighter to focus on defeating the enemy, however there is a very slight chance that they will die on duty, let alone at the hands of the enemy. Combat is not for everyone, heck, it's not for most but there are many jobs that are essential to America's success on the field of battle and these are as safe as any civilian job. I'm not saying we should have a conscription program like some countries do but most high school graduates struggle with what they want to do after graduation. Some feel that college is the "right" path after they graduate but for most Americans, this option is very hard, if not impossible, to come by. The military can open a world of opportunity that most people will never experience otherwise. Now, if you've seen "Full Metal Jacket" or "Platoon" or any other military movie you may be hesitant to sign up but, let me tell you that most military movies are not an accurate depiction of the military today. The two movies I mentioned were from the Vietnam era and the rules were significantly different than they are now. While basic training is a shock to most civilians, it's not even close to what it was in the past. It is still challenging and relatively unpleasant but it's not as demeaning, for the most part, as depicted in "Full Metal Jacket" and it only lasts a short time. Once it's done, you'll never have to endure anything like that again, if you don't want to. Other "war" movies, like Blackhawk Down, are retellings of battles that almost never happen, which is why they are compelling movies, because the men in those situations had to endure an extraordinary set of circumstances that 99% of military members will never experience. Movies like "Jarhead" are a little more realistic because it depicts the endless hours of "downtime" most military members experience when "deployed". This is what most of the military can expect from their active-duty time. Even those who are out patrolling on a regular basis are not guaranteed to encounter the enemy. I deployed ten times to combat zones and I can count on one hand the times I was actually in mortal danger. Of the other hundreds of missions I conducted, my unit either had such combat superiority that the enemy provided little to no resistance, or we exploited the element of surprise which allowed us to secure the objective before the enemy had a chance to react, or we simply didn't come across any enemy combatants at all. The friends of mine who were in some serious scrapes had to volunteer several times to even be in those situations. They had to volunteer to join the military, then for our job, then for jump school, then to attend selection to be in our specialized unit. Once in the unit their potential for encountering the enemy grew exponentially due to the nature of the mission of the unit we supported. If you compare the number of U.S. military deaths during the last 19 years to the number of U.S. military deaths in other wars, you'll find that the number is significantly lower. This is due to our leaders valuing the lives of military members much more than in the past. Even in the beginning we took precautions to avoid as many U.S. casualties as possible. This has not always been the case in America's war history. So, as you can see, it's not easy or common to actually be in harm's way or encounter the enemy to the level where your life would be in danger. Joining the military for its vast opportunity is a relatively safe proposition. One more quick thing about "higher education" opportunities in the military, you can go to college for free, or with tuition assistance (free money to take classes) while you are in the military and attain several degrees. I personally achieved an associate's, a bachelor's, and a master's degree while serving in the military which allowed me to transfer my G.I. Bill benefits to my daughter so her college is covered. There are so many more opportunities like this in the military. It's a far better option than crushing student loans or working a minimum wage job.

Getting Things Done

You may have heard the phrase "the squeaky wheel gets the grease" and it couldn't be truer. If you sit idly by and take the injustices that afflict you then you have no one to blame but yourself. Additionally, if you want something and you are waiting on someone else to approve it, or do their part to move the project forward, then you must act. Now, there is something to be said for being patient and waiting for the right time but, there is nothing wrong with checking back with the person periodically to find the status. If the person gives you a solid time/date when what you want will be ready then respect that deadline if you can. If you can't then you'll need to continue to negotiate. Give the person all the information surrounding the situation in a calm and respectful manner and you'll find that they are much more receptive than if you are belligerent or demanding. Even if you are completely in the right you must maintain your composure while fully explaining your situation. A person is much more receptive to someone who is respectful and composed and will usually help if they see you are right. I say "person" because there is always a point of contact, a human, who is handling your situation, it's not an unknown entity. These people have names and bosses and can be held accountable. However, these people also have feelings and pride and will be significantly less tolerant if they are challenged. There are countless "legal" ways to stonewall your effort and, if you choose the belligerent route, they will exercise all of them to prevent you from getting what you want. That being said, if you find that the person is simply being lazy or is intentionally obstructing your effort then it is time to politely go over them and speak to their supervisor/boss. When you speak to the next person in the chain, lay out your case in the same calm, polite, and respectful way you did originally. The person with whom you were speaking may not have had the authorization to help you but the higher you go the more power is wielded. The people at the higher levels also seem more receptive to your requests, perhaps because they are at that higher level and have more of a vested interest in the company? Either way, they could do more than those under them. The key to all of this is documentation. Ensure you obtain everyone's name and employee number at the very least. This information can be used with the next people in the chain to illustrate your efforts and the roadblocks you've encountered. This information can also be used to give kudos to those who did help you. I've never directly benefited from giving positive feedback to a customer service rep but maybe someone else has? Or maybe the actual rep benefited from it by having that feeling of satisfaction and accomplishment one does after receiving recognition from their chain of command. This also may prevent that rep, if they were having a bad day, from acting adversely to the next customer thereby passing on the positive energy? This action applies to all aspects of life from your child's school to a city council, to the office of the governor. No organization is without a chain of command populated by people who have different levels of authority. There is always a way to "get the grease" if you are tenacious enough. You must ensure the endeavor is worth your time and effort. But, if an injustice is being done, accepting your fate and doing nothing may result in someone else's plight in the future.

Public Speaking

Speaking in public is an extremely important task that you should be comfortable doing if you want to be successful. Now, when I talk about "public speaking" I'm not only referring to standing on a stage behind a lectern giving a prepared speech. There are many situations that require you to verbally express yourself to others and the more comfortable you are the better you'll be at conveying your information. This will result in a better chance of your audience receiving your message. You should address this issue like you should all issues, with excitement and enthusiasm because you have the opportunity to conquer a fear and grow stronger. You shouldn't shy away from things that make you uncomfortable or scare you. "Public" speaking is one of these issues that you can master and, just like everything, practice is the key to getting better.

The first step is to educate yourself on the source material. Know every aspect of what you're discussing and become a subject matter expert. One is never more confident at conveying information about a subject as when they know everything about it.

The next step is to put your speech together and practice. Start at home by yourself or with a roommate/family member and rehearse your "speech" until you can almost recite it from memory. Also, record yourself and watch it later to analyze your technique, it's very beneficial to observe yourself as your audience will. Check for nervous ticks, weird mannerisms, "fillers" or "speech disfluency", etc. Check for volume, flow, and coherency. Is what you're saying making sense? If not, why? Do you need to reword what you're saying? Your speech must be interesting and logical to ensure you don't lose your audience.

Once you hone this ability you should find ample opportunities to exercise it. Speak to whomever you can. Put yourself in situations where a conversation is warranted and natural and practice speaking clearly and confidently. You may feel awkward, or even silly at first but you'll eventually start to feel comfortable and you will stop thinking about doing it and simply do it. As you become more confident, look for opportunities to increase your audience. Volunteer to speak to a group of people in a social setting, lead a meeting at work, or testify before a school board or city council meeting. You should strive to reach a point where you can speak to anyone at any time about anything. It may seem like an unattainable task but as I said, the more you do something the better you become at it and the more comfortable you'll be doing it.

Being able to speak in public is imperative if you want to get what you want in life. If you are timid or apprehensive about speaking to someone about what you want or need then you will have a very difficult time obtaining it. This is not to say that you should be overbearing or untactful with your requests, on the contrary, your practice should entail speaking in a respectful and considerate way. One very important reason to be respectfully and professionally vocal in your life is that the person or entity with whom you need to speak might not be aware of your issue, request, or concern. Simply providing clear, concise, background information may result in a positive and timely solution. It's difficult for someone to help you if they don't know what you need or want.

Mastering the ability to convey your message clearly and convincingly is an invaluable skill that requires practice, courage, and above all else, confidence. You must give the impression that you know exactly what you're talking about while simultaneously being somewhat entertaining in order to capture and hold an audience's attention and properly convey your message.

Bullying

Let's talk about bullying. I'm not talking about physical bullying which has a simple, though not always easy, fix: tell someone. Physical bullying is a crime that should be dealt with as all crimes should, with involvement by the authorities. Verbal, cyber, and other "non-violent" bullying can be solved with a very simple solution: ignore the bully. We spend far too much time telling bullies not to bully when we should be focusing our time on instilling courage and toughness in "victims" – I put victim in quotes because someone who is being "non-violently" bullied is not a victim, they are simply someone who is allowing another human to have power over them. If they simply choose not to allow the bully to affect them then the bully is powerless and no longer a "threat" (not that they ever were.) What ever happened to "sticks and stones will break my bones, but words will never hurt me?" How did we get to a place where people are hurt by words? The truth is they aren't, they simply haven't been given the tools to deal with a non-violent bully. We need to focus our resources on educating kids on how to not let bullies get to them. Focusing on getting bullies to stop bullying is futile. Bullies don't feel like, or don't care, that they're bullying. No amount of "touchy-feely" safety stand downs is going to change that. Educating kids on not caring what others say about them is key. Explain to them that the bully is simply trying to upset them and no one with that goal should warrant their attention. This will take practice, perseverance, and support from everyone around the "victim." Once the "victim" has their mind right they won't be bothered at all and will no longer consider themselves a "victim". Now, this isn't to say that the "victim" shouldn't tell their parents, teachers, bus driver, etc. so the bully can be told to lock it up but, the more kids who ignore the "bully", or maybe even show them kindness, the better the chances that the bully will stop. But if the bully doesn't stop then you take his power away in other ways. But what you don't do is waste valuable school time with seminars or assemblies telling people not to bully others. Again, bully's either don't know or don't care that they are bullying someone. You can give them an example of how what they're doing isn't right and that they should stop but it will either fall on deaf ears or the bully will justify their actions or simply not care. You must empower those who feel defenseless, not hope to stop the offender. There will always be an offender, that seems to be an absolute certainty in this world, and the only way to be truly safe is to obtain the tools to defend yourself. Not

caring is one of the most powerful weapons a person can

wield.

Controlling Your Emotions

The aforementioned mindset isn't only valuable

with regard to bullies, it applies in many other situations.

There may be a time when someone says something that

unintentionally "hurts your feelings". You may get upset at

them for saying it, but I submit to you that no one can

actually hurt your feelings. You allow people to hurt your

feelings by caring about what they say. The simplest way

to combat this feeling is to not care what those people

think. Unfortunately, there are those people who you

respect whose words you will always care about. But

should you? If your friends/family say things that hurt your

feelings but aren't true or simply meant to hurt or keep you

down, then those opinions are no longer valid and must be

disregarded. However, if what they are saying is true and

their words are coming from a place of love and concern then you'll need to listen and correct the problems/issues. In order to differentiate between the two, you must be honest with yourself. Is what they are saying false? Is it true but they are saying it to try to make you feel bad, or guilty? Are they saying it sincerely in an attempt to help? Once you make this evaluation you must then be strong and either ignore the negativity or embrace the truth in order to make change in your life. Either way, you must decide that the information, whatever it is, will not get you down but will be used to build you up, to empower you, so you can ascend above this issue. The key to this is not blaming someone for "hurting your feelings" but owning what they say and controlling your emotions – not in a vindictive or disingenuous way, but truly control your emotions and refuse to let them affect your mood or disposition. Far too often I hear people say things like "he made me feel bad" or "he embarrassed me" etc. These statements are not true. No one can make you feel any way than you want to feel.

Yes, there will be that initial reaction to what has happened but that is you simply reacting to it and allowing that action to control you. You don't have to allow that feeling to grow, you can simply choose to not be upset, or sad, etc. When we allow a situation or person to control our emotions we lose control. The problem is that we don't want to stop the feeling because our subconscious is telling us to react a certain way and it's natural for us to give in to that feeling but, it's also easy to simply change your mind to something else as if you are changing the channel of a television or flicking off a light switch. It takes practice, and won't be easy, but the solution is simple: stop thinking, caring about, and/or succumbing to the feeling. Now, there may be a time when it is ok to surrender to the feeling such as crying at a funeral or laughing at a movie, etc., but there will be times when that reaction isn't appropriate and that's where you can exercise your power over your subconscious. The most important time to apply this control is when an adversary is attempting to intentionally control how you feel. It may be a bully who is trying to scare you or a co-worker trying to embarrass you, or a family member trying to make you feel guilty. These are the times when you must do nothing except flick that switch and ignore, or compartmentalize, that feeling. I say both because there will be times when you want to revisit an incident you have compartmentalized in an appropriate environment to address the feelings that result. There are also times when you must simply ignore the feeling altogether and disregard the offender completely. Again, as I've said elsewhere in this book, this is not a "trick" you use to simply "get by" but a genuine change of your mind and attitude. If you are just trying to put on a brave face to fool your foe then you are only fooling yourself and your adversary has actually won even though they might never know. You must flick the switch and genuinely not care. But this is not our goal, we couldn't care less about the person attempting to offend us, we only care about ascending and growing stronger. Hiding our emotions instead of controlling them is not conducive to ascension.

This can also be applied to "relationships", I use quotes because I'm not talking about relationships where two people feel mutual love and admiration/ for each other. I'm talking about someone pining over someone who either doesn't know the other person likes them or doesn't like the person back. It seems very selfish, and a little unstable, to crush on a person who has already told you they aren't interested - actually, this information should make the decision extremely easy. Why would anyone want someone who doesn't want them? That's the best part of a relationship, when you both want each other and no one else. That's the key, finding someone who loves you back, not someone who meets certain criteria, or a specific mold of what you are "looking for" in a mate. I realize there are some who are reading this and have no idea what I'm talking about because they got involved with someone for the wrong reasons or, not "wrong" because who's to say, but reasons other than the feeling of mutual admiration. If you are pining after someone right now, find the courage to tell that person, if they aren't interested then disregard them as they did you. Another one will come along. Or they won't. Either way, longing for someone who doesn't like you is a waste of time, time that could be spent bettering yourself.

Self-Awareness

I realize that many of the things mentioned in this book occur simply because we are not aware we are doing them. I think everyone's brain and self-awareness develops differently. I also believe self-awareness isn't something that just happens, I believe it is constantly evolving and increases with age. If you're like me, as you gain more and more self-awareness you look back at what you've done with a certain degree of embarrassment, a feeling of "did I actually do that?" It seems unimaginable the things we did when we were younger, like it wasn't even us and, to a certain extent, it wasn't. But that's the goal, to grow, to ascend to the next level and keep ascending throughout your life. Don't be embarrassed of the things you did, wore, or said. Think of them as events necessary for growth. Had these things not occurred then you might have been stuck on that lower plane. However, I also believe that some never learn from their past and continue on the same plane for their entire life. Even as I write this I realize that I have not ascended as far as I can. I believe I have more mental growing to do but I am open to it and accept it which, hopefully, will help me continue to ascend. Now, people may look at the word "ascend" as something cosmic or crazy but it's just a word to describe a person's increasing self, and situational, awareness. I address Situational Awareness later. There's nothing cosmic about it, it's simply a way to increase your joy in life. The joy that comes from acceptance of what happens and the power to process it and use it to your advantage.

What people fail to realize is that there are no rules in this life. Sure, there are laws that will keep you out of trouble/jail, but those laws were made by man. No rules apply, really. We make decisions to follow the rules/laws in the area in which we live in order to stay out of trouble and/or because it is the morally right thing to do. Aside from morally wrong acts, there are a ton of "socially acceptable" things that we are "supposed to do". Things that people expect us to do, that we absolutely do not have to do. Social norms and idiosyncrasies that make other people feel better or make situations more comfortable sometimes serve us better but that's not to say they are mandatory. Some other person's "comfort" is none of your business, it's on them to ascend and overcome their own insecurities. I don't ask for permission or acceptance for the things I do. We are all equal humans who answer to no one other than those to whom we choose. "We" create boundaries/rules that suit some/most of us but that's not to say you can't be who you want to be. However, if you choose to operate outside the "rules" don't be surprised when achieving your goals is more difficult. This isn't necessarily a bad thing; some need a challenge to find success while others are content with following the "rules" and having an "easy" life. Fortunately, you don't have to absolutely follow one or the other path, that's what I mean by no rules and freedom. If you find that following a societal norm will result in achieving your goal faster, then doing so may be the correct choice. Some think that absolute freedom is following no rules, but freedom includes deciding when you'd like to conform. Choosing to conform is different than being forced to conform. Some allow others to impose their will on them by reacting to judgment or "brow beating" but you must first empower a person for them to have that effect on you. As I've said, ignoring a person who is detrimental to your life is the most powerful weapon in your arsenal, it not only allows you to rise above the situation but also shows the other person that what they are saying is insignificant and has no power over you. When I say "ignore", that's exactly what I mean. I don't mean pretend to ignore, or ignore and then have the situation consume you later, I mean actually ignore what was said/done to the point where you not only stop caring but you forget about the situation all together. Training yourself to let things go is the greatest power of all. Too often people act like they don't care yet carry the burden in their mind which can be extremely heavy and will prevent any kind of ascension. Again, there is nothing cosmic about what I'm saying, and there's a simple solution – it requires you to let things roll off your back so you can drive on and leave the dead weight behind. BL: Never compromise unless you feel it necessary for your ascension.

Situational Awareness

Situational Awareness, or "SA", is being aware of your surroundings or your "situation" at all times. This is akin to not getting intoxicated to the point where you are unable to properly care for yourself. You should never be oblivious to your surroundings or location. You should always be at a degree of readiness of which you aren't necessarily physically ready to act but mentally aware so if you do have to physically act it won't require much effort to transition to physical action. It may seem exhausting at first but it's actually quite easy once you make it a part of your life. For instance, as I'll talk about in the "Military Experience" section, when you walk into a room, stop and take a few seconds to assess the room with all of your senses. Look for exits and their accessibility, assess the other occupants and determine their threat level. Listen for anything out of the ordinary, are there noises that don't fit this environment? Is someone yelling? Lastly, are there any weird odors? Usually this hits you right away, but they may be subtle and require a slightly heightened level of awareness until the oddity has been identified.

This isn't to say that you should never be hyper focused on something but, before you lose SA, you should ensure the environment is secure and most likely won't escalate to a situation where you'll need to move from mental awareness to physical action. This could be in your home with the doors locked, alarm on, dog present, etc. These precautions will allow you to focus on something else, and temporarily let your guard down, because if there is a threat, they will alert you and give you time to become mentally aware of your surroundings to make an informed decision on the level of physical action required, if any.

In addition to maintaining a certain level of awareness, it is also imperative to maintain a certain degree of unpredictability. Just think how incredibly hard it is to play defense all the time, constantly protecting something from a well-planned attack. This is what law enforcement, security details, etc. do continually, being ever vigilant against an "enemy" that has time to plan extensively against a known target. The main weapon these entities have against their enemies is unpredictability. If you fall into a pattern of life that allows an enemy to calculate and anticipate your next, and possibly every, move then you are vulnerable to "attack". I put attack in quotes because there are different levels of attack. Some attacks may be simple and only meant to slightly disrupt your life while others may be meant to completely upend it. Following a clandestine routine (one that only you and your family know) is a good way to keep your life in order but, depending on your level of vulnerability, you may want to consider altering your overt routine. If possible, change departure times from work, home, etc. Have lights on timers that turn on at different times of day and consider changing them periodically to discourage any would be attackers. Take different routes to and from work, home, the store, etc. Change up your schedule if possible. This can be challenging if you have children who have activities at the same time each day. If this is the case, perhaps solicit a friend to carpool (this will help in other ways too) or have your significant other pick up/drop off the kids some days. I realize that this all may seem extraneous, and that it may not apply to everyone, but it all depends on your station in life, neighborhood, vulnerabilities, etc. Now, this unpredictability doesn't have to be solely to thwart a criminal threat, there is also value in being unpredictable in your everyday life to prevent any unwanted conflict, large or small. Having a predictable schedule allows people to anticipate what you will do or where you will be which can have unfavorable, or even negative, effects on your life. Irregularity, coupled with selflessness and ambition, can have a strong effect on those around you. People will underestimate you which will work to your advantage. Those who actually need to know your full potential will, and everyone else will assume they know everything about you because of what you allow them to know. Unless they are your friends or family, it's not necessary to fully expose your true self to anyone. On the contrary, it may be a detriment to allow someone you can't trust to know too much about you because there is a risk that they may use that information against you.

The Hard Right over the Easy Wrong

Doing the Hard Right over the Easy Wrong means that, given the choice, choose to do what's correct and difficult instead of the wrong thing on the path of least resistance. This could be relative given a person's upbringing but, of the things a person knows is wrong, they should do the hard rights instead. This could be something as menial as putting off your laundry to do something fun resulting in you not having any clean clothes, leaving you scrambling to get squared away. It could also mean not preparing for the next morning the night before in order to mitigate the chances of flail (flail means not having anything squared away and having to run around hastily doing it – picture a frightened chicken running around a barnyard flapping it's wings). There is nothing more satisfying than being squared away and having everything ready to go before you do a fun/important thing - it makes the fun things significantly more enjoyable and allows for hyper focus on the important tasks ahead. Doing the right thing alleviates the anxiety of the looming, uncompleted task allowing you to relax and have fun or crush the important thing. While the easy wrong may seem "right" at the time (or, at least justified in some way), it is only delaying the inevitable and, the inevitable may be detrimental if not addressed properly.

Confidence

I've spoken about the pitfalls of someone else controlling your actions and this next part is another way we allow others to have power over us. I find it hard to believe how much time, money, and effort people waste on trying to impress others. Buying a certain article of clothing or possession for the sole purpose of trying to impress another is a form of weakness, especially when you really can't afford that item. When you place impressing others before being financially secure you need to reevaluate your life and come to the realization that it doesn't matter what people think of you if you are doing the right thing. Even if you can afford these items, caring what others think of you based on what you wear or what you own instead of your actions is wasteful and foolish. That's not to say you shouldn't look professional at work, or nice at a wedding, etc. but, those who have to look a certain way before they leave the house because they're worried about what people will think of them, are slaves. On the other hand, if you choose to dress a certain way because it makes you happy then you are free. Insecurity is a problem in this country that needs to be addressed. It can lead to issues from shyness to depression and has a relatively simple solution, growing stronger. Some people in my life don't like when I say that phrase because growing stronger requires effort when it would be much easier for others to change so we don't have to. But this isn't realistic, the only way to be truly free is to take control of your emotions and not allow external factors to negatively affect you. This can prove difficult. While you will always have the ability to do it, we are human, and we will succumb to the pressures of life and lose our mental step. However, it won't be forever, and the confidence will come back, usually after a deep breath or change of scenery. These bouts of weakness will become shorter and dealing with them will become reflexive as you become stronger. After time and practice, these bouts of weakness will subside all together allowing you to ascend even higher.

The main way to combat these feelings is to legitimately, truly, feel confident. I don't mean "act" confident; I mean actually be confident. There shouldn't be any lingering doubts in the back of your mind. These doubts are detrimental to your growth. Instead of "doubts", change these thoughts into reminders of what could happen and use them to move forward instead of letting them hinder your progress. Doubts are a detriment, but "reminders" are key to keeping you honest and on track. If we were to simply do whatever we wanted without checking ourselves against the reminders we would not be successful. We must be confident to make good decisions but allow the reminders of what could happen shape our decisions. Every decision should be prefaced by a series of "what ifs" to ensure you're making the best one. This process shouldn't take too long but it can take as long as you need. For me it's a very fast process that doesn't always encompass every scenario but enough to make an informed decision. As the importance of the decision grows, so should the length of time you spend on "what ifs". Let your mind flow as you transition, hypothetically, from scenario to scenario and know that it's not exactly a tangible progression but a free-thinking method that allows you to explore several possibilities. Always try to think three to four steps ahead and attempt to anticipate as many hypothetical scenarios as possible to ensure you eliminate as many potential issues as you can. For instance, if I want to buy something, I assess if I have enough money, if I will actually use the item, will buying the item take away from something else I might want later? If it does, am I ok with that? Where will I keep it? Etc. This process takes seconds to complete and eventually will be almost involuntary. If you apply this process to everything you do (within reason and proportion) you should be more successful than if you "wing it."

In addition to this free-thinking technique, seeking advice is also very beneficial to your growth. I tell my kids that they should listen to everything people say and then sift through the information to determine what can be used now, later, or not at all. Some people have a hard time taking advice because they either don't respect the person from whom the advice originated, or they don't want anyone telling them how to live their life. I struggled with this for a long time. I wanted to do everything myself, many times resulting in a negative effect. But it felt like I was either being told what to do, which I hated (still kinda do), or "cheating" in some way because I didn't figure out a solution on my own. The latter reason is hard for some because they lose focus on what life's about, which is happiness. If following the advice of someone else will result in your success (read: happiness) then you should get past yourself and take the advice. Now, since the ultimate goal is happiness then you must ensure that heeding someone else's advice will actually result in your happiness and not stew inside you causing you more grief than when you began. People achieve happiness in different ways and, if compromising your ideals will result in your sorrow, then sticking to yourself may be your best bet since you won't be able to enjoy any success that is given and not earned. I will submit to those who think this way that it can be liberating to have others "make decisions" for you. Having been in the military for a large chunk of my life, I was afforded many opportunities to be told what to do and it wasn't always bad. In fact, I owe a great deal (if not all) of my success to the men and women I've worked with in the military. When you are given "guidance" it allows you to simply execute without having to do much of the planning. You still reap the benefits without putting in the work. Now, obviously this isn't always a good thing, some people in your life will attempt to manipulate you into doing something that appears to be beneficial to you but ultimately benefits them a great deal more. If the amount of success you achieve is acceptable then there's no issue allowing them to profit as well but, you have to ensure they are not taking advantage of you.

Another sandbag that can hinder your ascension is constantly complaining about the issues that are preventing you from rising. These issues could have to do with your body, a relationship, self-esteem, etc. Whatever they are, you must decide if you want to change these problem areas or accept them and be happy with who you are. My suggestion, obviously, is to self-evaluate and determine why these issues are occurring. Are they present because you lack motivation? Do you have an injury? Are you just being lazy? You must be honest with yourself and, if your issues are self-generated, then you must own your shortfalls and work to eliminate them, or at least minimize them. Along with all the things I mention in this book, "fixing" the things about yourself within your control is extremely liberating and satisfying. Along the same lines, letting go of the things you can't control is also freeing and therapeutic. I don't mean pretending that you don't care in front of others. Publicly over-exaggerating and accentuating your indifference yet harboring shame privately manifests itself in tears, overeating, and self-harm. Usually when people accentuate their indifference about something they are overcompensating and don't really feel that way. Don't be that person. Own what you can control and let go of what you can't. It's simple, easy, and very doable.

The main thing you must remember in life is no matter where you are, what you're doing, or how ignorant you are of what's going on, you must have the confidence to walk into any situation like you own the place. Be confident and know that you are making every effort to do the noble and righteous thing and do not be discouraged by anyone or anything. Not knowing is not the same as being scared. Confidence is handling that ignorance correctly. If you cower at the challenge and fail to seek out the knowledge that will allow you to prevail then your journey will be long and arduous but, if you lean forward and attack the situation, the answers you seek will reveal themselves.

Organization

The best way to keep your life simple and easy is to become organized. Know where everything is and put everything back in its place. The most common thing that comes to mind is car keys/wallet/etc., why are these things always so hard to find? Because people don't put them back in the same place every time, they feel like it's too restricting when in reality it is a colossal time saver and mind easer (see the section on doing the Hard Right over the Easy Wrong). I wonder how much time and effort is wasted looking for things people use every day? Seems like an easy kill. Some people who live in clutter and disorganization think they "have a system" and that their clutter is organized chaos, but I'll bet if those same people were to become organized their productivity would increase significantly. If you make a plan (don't fall in love with it, as I cover elsewhere in this book), stick to a routine (for the basic things), and keep your house/office decluttered, you will be able to focus on what's important instead of the "mess" that is perpetually in front of you. Hang up/put away your clothes, put your shoes in the same place every time, etc. If you streamline the easy stuff, you'll free up gray matter for more important things. By minimalizing distractions, you can focus on what's truly

important. I can give you more ideas regarding

organization based on your unique situation. Just shoot me

an email describing your situation and we'll come up with a

solution: jarrod@tryitlikethis.net.

Email

Speaking of organization, if possible, never delete

any emails. If you're using Microsoft Outlook, make an

Outlook Data File somewhere it won't be accidently, or

intentionally, deleted and then create folders for all the

emails. You can make a folder for each person you

encounter, or for a certain subject/project, etc. If you're

using a web-based email like Gmail, simply make folders

and save the emails in the appropriate folder. Having said

this, do most of your important work via email to ensure

documentation. If people insist on using the phone and not

following up with an email it may be that they either can't

type, or they are covering for themselves to ensure

plausible deniability which indicates an integrity issue. In these instances, you must insist their guidance, instruction, adherence, and/or concurrence be in writing to ensure you are covered.

<u>"Multitasking"</u>

Some people feel the need to "multitask" because they are concerned that if they concentrate on one thing for too long, they may lose focus on what else needs to get done or another project that must be completed. So, they do a little of each project at the "same time" and do none of them well. Making a prioritized list will help with this endeavor. Prioritizing your "to do" list enables you to focus on the most important things first and not get distracted by things that are either not important or "due" after the other items at the top of your list. The future items may be more "important" but if tackling them can wait while you take care of some smaller or less important tasks, then it can provide that ease of mind and happiness for which we all strive. Write down everything that needs to get done to free your mind and focus on the task at hand. This will allow you to perform each task in a timely and professional manner. This also leaves you freedom to switch from task to task without having to focus on other tasks because they are already written down and documented for future reference. Make prioritized "to do" lists often. Put them in a place you will see them. Make them organized and neat so they do not become an eye sore but actually help. If items on the lists keep getting transcribed to new lists, you must decide if those items will ever get done and decide if they are OBE (overcome by events). This means that your situation has changed and negates the need for those items, and they should be removed. If, after serious evaluation, you determine that this item is important and should stay on the list then keep it otherwise, get rid of it. The list can be anything, a sticky note, your phone, or an email to yourself. A quick note about emailing a reminder, if it is something that is always changing, or needing updated, simply reply to the previous email reminder to have a running archive of the project details. You can also text to your email which comes in handy if you don't have time to draft an email. As I alluded to in the email section, I suggest email be the main source because you can save your emails to folders for better organization. Back to multitasking, or not multitasking. Again, if you want to do a job well then focus on that job and nothing else. I would suggest keeping the impeding distractions to a minimum or eliminate them all together. These distractions could be the television, spouse, children, radio, etc. Some are actually more productive when music is playing but you must make that decision and be honest about it. There are times when I don't have to focus too much on the job at hand, but it takes a lot of "grunt" work to complete so I turn on the tunes to drone out and plug away at the task. On the other hand, if I really need to concentrate, I have to be honest with myself and turn off the music, keep it low, or turn on music that is not distracting. I would steer clear of podcasts or talk radio because, as boring as some find it, it is still a distraction. Regardless of how boring it may seem, it's just human nature to wonder what is being said within ear shot. You just have to find an environment that is the most conducive to maximizing your productivity and insist on it.

Fitness

It's one of the craziest things; food tastes awesome yet if you eat too much it's a detriment to your body. Fast food, sugar, beer, etc. is in high demand and makes billions each year. Billions. Fast food makes over half a trillion dollars, the beer industry makes about 100 billion dollars, and, since sugar is in everything, who knows how much they make each year. The point is, the U.S. population is growing, and not just the number of people but also the size of the actual people. Now, I believe in capitalism, freedom, and personal responsibility so I am in no way blaming these industries for our country's obesity problem. I am simply illustrating some of the root causes of that obesity. I've eaten/drank my fair share of all of the aforementioned items, and still do on occasion, but I've done so less and less over time. I think the main reason I have decreased my intake of these items is because I am trying to be as fit as possible and ingesting these items is a direct detriment to that goal. What sucks is that it takes so little of these food items to negate a lot of fitness activity. But we can cry about it or we can be intellectuals and rise to a different plane of existence and realize that those items are unnecessary and that there are so many other joys in life that are hindered by these already harmful items. I don't even think I'm fully there yet mentally. I have cravings like everyone else and I either cave (not nearly as much as I used to) or, more often than not, I hold myself accountable and think about how weak it is for anything to have control over me. I used to smoke, chew tobacco, drink more than I should, etc. and these were relatively easy to quit because they, unlike food, do absolutely nothing for your body –

they only hurt it. Take hangovers, for example. I can't see myself ever drinking any significant amount of alcohol again let alone an amount that would give me a hangover. Food, on the other hand, can be rationalized as essential for survival and usually "bad" food is cheaper and more accessible than "good" food. So, eating correctly is probably the hardest thing to do out of all the things I mentioned. The key is to first get your mind right. When I say this I don't mean "tricking" yourself into not wanting the food, or not eating the food and then agonizing about it, I mean actually coming to the realization that you don't need the bad food and that eating it would hinder what's actually important. You must rise above the cravings and the weakness and change the way you see food. That's not to say you can't find good tasting "good" food and, when you do start eating correctly, you'll find that the "bad" food doesn't taste as good and it certainly won't sit very well with your body. Your body will grow accustomed to eating right and will reject the "bad" food. But getting your mind right is the first step. Once you honestly outgrow the weakness of cravings they will no longer have any control over you. "Bad" food will no longer be an option for you. If you think of food as fuel, and not a pastime or hobby, you'll be less apt to binge eat or eat the wrong thing. Again, it's a mindset and ascension to a plane of existence that doesn't give in to irrational feelings like cravings. There are so many more fulfilling and meaningful things to do in this life that don't have anything to do with eating. A sedentary lifestyle is easy and comforting. We can sit in front of our TVs or on our phones and relax and not worry about our problems but, does this eliminate our problems? No. As I mention elsewhere in this book, there is nothing more satisfying than achieving a goal or completing a task that has been on our mind. So, not only is a sedentary lifestyle not conducive to ascending but it also contributes to our descension. We aren't really relieving stress or "decompressing" by watching TV or our phones, we're masking our problems with distractions. This isn't to say you shouldn't blow off things you can't control. If there is a certain problem that you can't do anything about then find a healthy distraction to either take your mind off the problem or help you focus on a solution. I'm not saying that you shouldn't do things that are unproductive or frivolous, you absolutely should do these things but, don't include eating in that list of activities.

Eating right alone isn't optimal. Exercise is imperative if you want to achieve your best health. Exercise is defined as "activity requiring physical effort, carried out to sustain or improve health and fitness." This doesn't necessarily mean running for miles or going to the gym, it simply means not being sedentary. Ideally your choice of exercise will be something you enjoy. This is why most fail to achieve their goals, they are exercising in a manner that not only isn't enjoyable but isn't even tolerable. They set themselves up for failure. If you choose an activity that you don't mind, or even enjoy, doing you'll find the time to exercise. You may also choose to do little things throughout the day like take the stairs, stand instead of sit, or volunteer to restock the paper when the resupply arrives.

Some say that they can't exercise because of an injury but that is often not true. When I was in the military, and sustained an injury, the doctor would write me a waiver that specified what I could and could not do. In addition to rehabilitating the injured area, if I had a lower body injury then he would prescribe upper body only exercises. Upper body injury? Lower body only. We use things as excuses in order to be comfortable but sometimes (most times) the right answer is to, safely, leave your comfort zone. Most refer to the comfort zone as a mental or emotional place, but it can also be your physical comfort zone. Elite athletes leave their physical comfort zone to achieve greatness, you can do the same. In order to excel you must push your body to work harder than you're used to and sometimes harder than you think it can handle. Your body can do significantly more than your mind thinks it can. I mentioned doing all of this safely, meaning don't push so hard that you either reinjure yourself or sustain a new injury but, don't quit so early that you aren't able to improve. Doing all of this under the guidance of a professional is a good idea but we are all in tune with our own bodies and can tell when we've reached our max. That's how our brain gets in the way, it quits too early and doesn't allow our body to achieve our goals. You must find that point where you can shut off your conscious mind and let your subconscious take over. This is not easy, it's something you have to work up to but elite athletes, soldiers, etc. have put themselves through enough training where they know their limitations and know when they can surpass them. Now, do you as someone who is simply trying to be healthy need to put yourselves through the anguish of pushing yourself to your absolute limit? Probably not but, you should at least push yourself farther than you've been. If you're a walker, try holding some weight while you walk, or wear a weight vest, or climb

some hills. If you're a jogger/runner, try to decrease your

time at a given distance or increase your distance at a given

time or sprint the last 30 seconds or minute of your run.

You'll find that pushing yourself, even a little bit, will feel

awesome and it'll make you want to do more. This

euphoric feeling is what drives people to push themselves.

One of the techniques I've used to shut off my brain to

allow my body to take over is, obviously, music. Music is

probably the most common distraction people use because

of its motivational properties. Another way to shut off your

mind is to occupy it with other thoughts. What are you

going to do later that day? What are you having for a meal

when you get done working out? What's a good way to

improve your kids' futures? You get the idea. Anything

you can do to occupy your mind so it can forget about what

your more than capable body is doing. The absolute worst

thing most people can do is focus on what they're doing. If

you are hyper aware of exactly what you're doing you are

more than likely focusing on how much it sucks and how much you want it to be over. Now, if you choose an activity that you love, you don't have to worry about any of this. You will be having such a great time in your activity that you won't mind putting out the amount of effort required to get a good workout.

Why should you work out? Why can't you just eat the right foods and the right number of calories to maintain your optimal weight? Your body is growing weaker as you grow older and to maintain or increase your strength and endurance (not just cardiovascular endurance but also the endurance, or durability, of your bones, organs, etc.), physical exercise is necessary. Cardiovascular (cardio) exercise will work your heart and lungs, weight-bearing exercises will increase bone density, etc. so, diet alone isn't the best way to stay healthy for the long haul. Some people say "who cares? We're all gonna die anyway, why not enjoy yourself?" But are you really enjoying yourself? For every minute of gluttony, how many hours of discomfort do you suffer? My father used to take medicine before each meal because the food he chose to eat gave him heartburn and I always wondered why he would continue to do something that caused him pain. That's a real problem in this country, taking medication instead of living correctly. Why not eat correctly and live well so you don't have to take medication? Healthcare is always a hot button issue in this country because very few people take care of themselves. If more people ate correctly and exercised, there would be less need for healthcare and our medical professionals could focus on those who actually need care instead of those who need care because they have not been taking care of themselves. However, this isn't what pharmaceutical companies and hospital administrators want. Money does strange things to people. When these companies are doing well, they want more money but not as much as when they are struggling. Either way, they don't care about you so, it is in your best interest to care about yourself, and for yourself. So, eat correctly (most of the time), exercise (at least moderately), and do things that make you happy (as much as you can.) It's very simple but not easy. You must burn more calories than you take in to achieve weight loss. If you're at your target weight then you can simply eat an equal amount to what you burn however, you should be exercising so you'll need more calories to account for the amount you burn when exercising. "Listen" to your body. It'll tell you when you're hungry and when you're not. It'll tell you what sits right with you and what doesn't. A lot of us refuse to listen to what our body is telling us, and we suffer for it. There are all types of conditions now that never used to be around. Well, they were around, we just didn't name them. If you can't eat dairy, or have trouble with bread, etc. then you need to listen to your body and stop eating them. Make substitutions, eat things that are healthy but also don't cause you any ill feelings. Pay attention to how you feel after you eat, is the food sitting right with you? Did you eat too much? If you find yourself consistently overeating (feeling bloated or uncomfortable after a meal) then eat slower next time since it takes some time for your body to feel like it's full. If you wolf down your food, eat more, and then feel horrible after, it's probably because you ate too fast and your stomach didn't have time to tell your brain it had had enough. You can also alleviate this problem by portioning out your food based on how many calories you should be eating, but this can be a bit tedious if you're not into it. Some people love counting calories and do it religiously. If you are one of these people, there are plenty of apps that will scan UPC codes on food items and enter the nutrition data into the app to tell you how much you can eat based on how many calories you need. I try to stay away from saying things like how many calories you "can" have. This sounds like it's not your choice, but it absolutely is, and if you want to have more you can, if you want to have less, that's ok too. Above all else take ownership of your life in every way, to include your diet. If you understand this, you will have no problem achieving your goals because you are in control. Now, if you're the type of person who can't be trusted to achieve your own goals and you need a coach, contact me, I can help. I can be that motivation to help you achieve your goals. I can hold you accountable and redirect you to keep you on track.

Another important thing about staying "fit" is to get on a semi-rigid schedule and make it part of your life. Get up the same time every day and go to bed the same time every day. Make working out an appointment on your calendar that you must attend every day – schedule other things around it. You do have a calendar, right? If you have a phone you have a calendar. Make reminders in your phone's calendar, contact me if you aren't sure how to do it. I get reminders all day long about things I need to do, this alleviates the need for me to remember everything I must do. Do your best to adhere to your schedule. After all, you made the schedule for you, it doesn't make sense to get upset about having to do something you know is right for you, especially since you dictated it. You're an empowered person who decides what you're going to do so, do it. The calendar is your friend and will help you stay on track. Can you blow it off occasionally? Sure, but remember that the more you blow it off the easier it becomes and the more off track you'll be. Luckily, it doesn't matter how far off-track you go, you can always get back on. If you stay up late watching a movie, going on a date, seeing friends, etc., it's no problem but, make up for it the next day if you can. Sleep in, drink water, eat correctly, exercise...get back on track. People think they are missing out by not going out all night, or drinking alcohol/using drugs, etc., but I say they are missing out on truly meaningful experiences by abusing their body with things that have absolutely no benefit. They put themselves "behind the power curve" meaning they'll have to work even harder to make up for the mistakes they made. The goal is to ascend, you can't ascend if you keep intentionally descending.

Years ago, I decided to stop drinking. I don't advertise it (aside from this book) and I certainly don't tout it at parties, etc. I don't do it because I simply don't like the after affects alcohol has on my body socially, physically, and mentally. Like tobacco and drugs, I simply don't see the point. It all boils down to this and this is what you should be asking yourself before you do anything detrimental to yourself: "what's the point?" "Am I getting anything at all out of this?" Some people will say "a good time" or "lower inhibitions so I can actually speak to people without anxiety", etc. to which I say, grow stronger! Don't be a slave to drugs or alcohol. Rise above the fear of social interaction and be intelligent enough to have a good time without being "messed up". I digress. People treat alcohol like it's not just another drug, but it is. Alcohol has the same, if not worse, negative effects on people's lives as any other drug. More people die from alcohol than all other drugs combined. Alcohol is the third leading preventable cause of death in the country, yet people treat it like it's not harmful at all and actually celebrate its consumption. I'm not saying that you shouldn't have the right to drink if you choose but I don't see why anyone interested in health would. I also don't understand that, if more people die from alcohol than all other drugs combined, why aren't other drugs legal? Because it would be worse if they were? Debatable. As I said, some people will say they drink to have "a good time" or "lower their inhibitions" but we have inhibitions for a reason, to keep us out of trouble! Seems like very flawed logic to do something knowing it will assist in bad decisions. If you can't function in society unless you've consumed alcohol or drugs, then you should put yourself in those situations more often when you're sober so you can get comfortable doing them. If you are intoxicated when you do the things from which your inhibitions are trying to protect you then you have a greater chance of making poor decisions regarding an already unfavorable set of circumstances. If you have your wits about you when you encounter these situations you are more apt to make correct decisions and ascend even higher. That's why addiction doesn't make sense to me. Yes, I understand that people try to "chase the high" but they know that they'll never feel as good as they did the first time they did the drug and, the more they do the drug, the worse they will feel when they stop so, do they plan to be high until they die? Why not suck it up, accept the withdrawals, and kick the habit altogether? While I've never taken any drug harder than marijuana, I have consumed a great deal of caffeine and sugar and I can tell you that those two "drugs" (which is essentially what they are) are as addicting as any other drug. The withdrawals from both caffeine and sugar are as debilitating as anything and it is absolutely miserable to stop either one of them, especially abruptly or "cold turkey". Not everyone has the time for recovery or strength to quit cold turkey, so a gradual weaning period might be better for some (those whose quitting cold turkey could be fatal, for instance) but the goal should be to stop. What do people do (or supposed to do) when they are hungover? Do they hope the pain continues? No, they sleep, drink water, eat right, etc. in the hopes that the pain goes away as quickly as possible. Others use the "hair of the dog" method, which is effective at first, I guess, but ultimately is unsustainable. Yes, the "experts" will tell you that it's not that easy and that people like me simply don't understand the intricacies and layers involved with addiction but that is just the industry and institution perpetuating their jobs. An overabundance of emotion and empathy are also a serious hindrance to a person's recovery. These "professionals" think that coddling and enabling are the way to stop a person from continuing their erroneous path but there must be a certain degree of realistic and sensible treatment that wakes the addicts so they can realize what they are doing to themselves. There is a reason why people choose to continue to use drugs to the point where it's a detriment to their life and, once that reason is identified then they can overcome the weakness. There is also something to be said about this being America where a person is free to do whatever they want to themselves as long as it doesn't hurt anyone else. By "hurt" I mean physically, not the mental anguish a family member feels when they are dealing with a loved one who is addicted to drugs or alcohol. I mean that we are free to do what we want as long as our actions are not a detriment to someone else's happiness. Some will argue that a person's addiction is contributing to their family's unhappiness, and this may be true, but this is not the "fault" of the addicts. The addict's actions are not legally a direct detriment to anyone else's life. Those affected by an addict's actions will disagree but, ultimately, this is America, and we are all free to do whatever we want provided it doesn't infringe on another's rights. Granted, the "law" prohibits certain drug use, but the "law" doesn't seem to be working. If an American wants to waste their gift of life, not grow stronger, and not ascend to a higher level of thinking and enjoy their gift, so be it. Who are we to say what they can or can't do with their life?

Finances

Do not accumulate "bad" debt or, debt you cannot repay each month or at all. There is very little financial education in today's society and children often enter adulthood with little to no information regarding debt and how to avoid accumulating too much of it. This is unfortunate because lenders prey on young people and don't really care if you amass a lot of debt because if you aren't able to pay off the debt then you accrue interest which means you not only pay what you owe but extra money for not paying your debt on time. The best course of action is to not amass any debt at all, if you can. The only debt that seems acceptable when you're young is a car loan but, when you're young your credit isn't established yet and you may not be able to secure a good interest rate.

If you borrow money from someone and don't pay it back right away, they charge you interest, or extra money on top of what you owe. This is how they make money. They are counting on you not paying off the loan and continuing to make payments for much longer than you would if there were no interest. They love those who can only pay the minimum payment because there is a good chance that the high interest rate will result in that person never paying down the loan or taking an exorbitant amount of time to do so, which results in more money in the lender's pocket. It would be significantly better if you could take public transportation, ride your bike, or walk until you acquire enough money to buy a car with cash, or enough for a substantial down payment to decrease your monthly payment and balance. This isn't to say that you shouldn't have credit cards or another form of credit because you need these things to increase your credit rating. The better your credit rating the more likely you'll be able to get the best interest rates and pay lower finance charges on car loans, home loans, credit card balances (which you shouldn't have for more than a month and won't have to worry about since you'll pay off your balance each month.) Now, there are extenuating circumstances where you might need to carry a credit card balance more than a month and, in those cases, you need to be frugal and have a plan to pay the balance as soon as possible. This means sacrifice (only using your money for necessities) and diligence. I can't stress enough how harmful it is to have an outstanding credit card balance. Everyone wants everything right now but, there are so many things you can do that cost little to no money that are actually good for you. Don't feel like you have to spend money to live your life. Have fun while being smart with your money so you can be financially independent as soon as possible.

Passive and/or residual income. The goal, as far as I'm concerned, is to try to generate as much passive/residual income as you can. Passive income is earned from rental properties, etc. and residual income is money you earn long after the initial investment or work. Real estate, books, YouTube videos, etc. can all generate income after you've already put in the work. If you generate enough passive/residual income streams, you'll no longer need to have a job and can focus on things you enjoy. This isn't to say that you couldn't also work and make even more money, it would be up to you at that point. This is the freedom to which I was referring earlier in the book. The freedom to live your life exactly how you want with nothing and nobody telling you anything different; to do what you want, when you want. This doesn't mean you have to be "rich"; it simply means you have to have enough money to live the way you want.

It can be nerve racking to worry about what might happen in your life. Having enough money in the bank/mattress/mason jar to cover these uncertainties can give you peace of mind. Peace of mind could mean several different things depending on your situation. If you rent your home, own your car (and it's in good condition), and have minimal bills then you might not need as much on hand as someone else, but you should still have about six month's salary in the bank at any given time. I know this seems like a lot, but it can be done over time and, once you have that "security blanket" you'll feel a lot more comfortable. Life is uncertain and having money set aside for emergencies like unexpected medical bills, car repairs, home emergencies, etc. will provide you with that peace of mind necessary to live happily. It may seem like a waste to keep money in an account "just in case" but you'll be glad you did if something catastrophic happens. Remember that the money isn't just "sitting" in the bank, it is accruing interest and making you even more money.

Communication

People often confuse talking with communication. Without listening, and understanding, communication doesn't work. If someone misinterprets what you say because they didn't understand what you meant, then it's up to you to clarify or restate the thought in a different way so that they can understand. Too often communication breaks down due to a lack of effort on the part of the sender. This break down could be caused by a lack of, or abundance of, intelligence. You may not know how to convey your message so someone else can understand because either you or the receiver lack the proper intellect. This isn't to say that either of you are not intelligent in your own right but there may be an issue of lacking intelligence on the particular subject. This also isn't to say that your receiver doesn't lack a certain degree of intelligence causing them to not understand but, it is still up to the sender to provide the information in a way that the receiver can comprehend the message. In addition to innocently not understanding a message, there are those people who intentionally misinterpret or assume the most offensive connotation behind your message. They do this because they are either indignant, want to be incensed to feed some need to play the victim, or attempting to demonize you. That seems to be the popular thing at the time of this writing, "catching" people saying something they either didn't mean or taking what they say out of context. Granted, there are people who should be exposed for the horrible people they are but, if a person misspeaks or is taken completely out of context and the "whistleblower" gets it wrong, then the whistleblower should be held accountable.

Anxiety

Anxiety often stems from things like uncertainty and procrastination. If you're uncertain, become certain by researching the subject and becoming an "expert". There is nothing more calming than confidence. The confidence in knowing that you have properly prepared for whatever endeavor you are attempting. Confidence is the feeling that you are going to crush, and nothing will prevent you from achieving your goal. Too often we put off preparation until the last minute leaving us no time to absorb the information. This leaves us feeling unsure of our ability to complete the task. As I say elsewhere, practice is the key to success. Preparation is just another form of practice and is vital to your success. As your knowledge of the given subject matter increases, your anxiety decreases. You may not fully overcome your anxiety about the project due to natural nervousness, but the feeling won't be debilitating and will actually assist in your endeavor. The feeling of apprehension will be replaced by excitement because you will want to share your preparation with others.

Another form of anxiety people struggle with is building up a situation in their minds and/or making the stakes too high to the point where they can't function or properly perform during that situation. Whether it be a job interview, a big test, or Thanksgiving dinner, you must minimize the importance of the event enough to perform at your full potential. If you feel that the situation is bigger than you then you will react accordingly. If you "own' the situation and actually adopt the mindset that you deserve to be there, and that you are better than the situation, you instill enough confidence in yourself to excel. If you allow the situation to overwhelm you then you not only have to perform with anxiety, but you'll have the lurking feeling that you don't belong there. This will fill your head with doubt, and doubt is the enemy of success. Doubt is different than caution, however and both are different from preparation. You want to face every situation so overly prepared that the task almost seems futile because you are so ready. Most anxiety stems from ill preparedness. Unfortunately, being prepared for a situation takes time and most people are not willing to take the time to properly prepare. They either think they won't need it, or that it's a waste of time if they don't actually achieve the goal, or they're just lazy.

Lastly, another way to minimize your stress and relax is to have contingency plans. Some people enter a situation thinking that if it doesn't work out then all will be lost but, if you have a "plan B" (and C, and D, etc. if possible) then the pressure can be alleviated because everything won't hinge on the moment at hand. Have a scenario or scenarios in mind that will guarantee that you will be fine if the deal doesn't go through. Some say that you must take risks to get what you want but those risks don't have to be showstoppers if they don't pan out.

If you need to get things done, then get them done. Don't procrastinate - It's weird, there is no worse feeling than knowing something needs to get done and there's no better feeling than getting something accomplished, yet we put things off until the last minute or blow them off altogether. The task might not even be that important, but the mental relief is. Do the menial tasks if for no other reason than to achieve peace of mind. If you feel like you should do something, whether it be a chore or a life changing event, do it. Don't wait for the "right time" because there is rarely ever a "right time" and the feeling of relief and accomplishment you get from doing that thing far outweighs the feeling you get from blowing it off. The feeling of something looming over you takes a greater toll than you realize and negatively affects your entire life without you really knowing it. The same is true about not procrastinating – that feeling you get when you accomplish something armors you against life's negative effects.

Be Present and Don't Settle

Take advantage and/or enjoy the situation at hand, don't look for the next thing and miss what's in front of you. That being said, don't settle if the thing in front of you is not fulfilling your goals or making you as happy as possible. Enjoy what you have but never settle, the experience isn't horrible but why not try to achieve everything you want? The worst is you are left with a slightly less pleasant situation. Never settle for miserable. If you absolutely can't stand your life, as a whole, then change it. If both your home life and work life are horrible then make a change. Don't waste any more time in the misery. On the other hand, if one of those is awesome then count your blessings, not everyone has one or the other and a lot of people don't have both. This isn't to say that you should settle if you don't have to. People think they are "stuck" where they are in life but that's simply not the case. You must be strong enough to make the change. You can do it, it just takes a bit of effort, and probably some sacrifice but the happiness will be worth it.

Criticism

I find it hard to believe that people still get upset over criticism. Criticism, in any form, should be welcomed and used to one's advantage. Your skin should be thick enough to listen to criticism, sift through the BS, find the gem (or gems) of truth to which you must adhere, and disregard the rest. While a simple concept, this can prove to be very difficult. If someone is attempting to legitimately correct your erroneous actions, you should welcome it for this will allow you to ascend quicker. If you deny the truth because it comes from someone you dislike, or do not respect, then it is to your own detriment. Some people don't like to adhere to advice from anyone other than those whom they feel are worthy of their time. This is an arrogant, and costly, way to live. I have learned a great deal from those I respect but I have also learned an equal amount from those who I not only didn't respect but downright despised. Alas, truth is truth, and to deny that is a hindrance to your ascension. In the military we were blunt and truthful when debriefing our peers, just as we expected them to be with us. We would actually get upset if no one had any constructive criticism because no one is perfect and if no one had any inputs that meant they weren't paying attention. We can't grow or ascend if we don't receive input from outsiders telling us where we can improve. We should welcome the feedback, regardless of the form in which it's presented. Some can't handle feedback unless it's presented in a certain way, usually in a way that doesn't "hurt" their feelings but, if you can't handle harsh feedback regarding your poor performance, how can you handle the real, brutal world? We should all strive to encounter adversity instead of shying away from it. The more adversity and strife we are exposed to the stronger we become. Some say this will cause us to be less nice but, again, this is a decision you make not an absolute certainty. It is possible to receive harsh feedback and still reply with respect and amiability – I did it often when I was a young airman. The key is to not become emotional when receiving feedback. Take it for what it is, a chance to grow stronger and ascend.

Chapter 2

Military Experience

I would say that I had an above average military career. I was able to work with the most elite units our country has to offer, and I learned a great deal from them. I wouldn't say I was as highly trained as them, not from a lack of trying but opportunities weren't as abundant for me and my guys as they were for our "customers" (what we called those elite units to which we were "attached"). However, we were highly trained in our own right and that training has residual effects that carried over into civilian life. For example, like I stated before, most people walk into a situation (like a store, their home, or work) and take their safety for granted whereas guys in my line instinctively assess the room for threats, exits, or anything out of the ordinary. This is done without thinking, like a reflex and, once the threats have been identified and egress points noted, we continue with our primary purpose, like grabbing a taco, buying groceries, or watching a swim meet.

Skewed Views

This military experience has also skewed my view of many things. The main one that comes to mind is the outdoors. I'm not sure how many others share this outlook but the first thing I do when someone points out a beautiful nature scene is assess how hard it would be to walk through it. I've walked in just about every type of terrain you could imagine: jungle, desert, swamp, mountains (both temperate and arctic conditions), tundra, etc. and usually with a rucksack weighing more than I liked. When exposed to these scenes I immediately, without realizing I'm doing it, wonder if I will be able to get a good stride going or will I hindered by "wait a minute" vines. Will I continually stumble over tussock, or resort to using my hands to ascend the grade? I also immediately think about what would happen if I was stuck in those environments, do I have enough food and water, cold weather gear, and/or personal protection? Many of the aforementioned terrains have four legged "OPFOR" (opposition force) who may or may not be hungry. These experiences have made it a tad difficult to see the beauty at times but, once I realize I don't have to walk up/around/through it, the beauty comes to the forefront.

Fight the Enemy, Not the Plan

Another very important thing I learned in the military is to fight the enemy, not the plan. What I mean by this is to make a plan but don't fall in love with it. It is unrealistic to think that a plan will be executed perfectly and rarely do plans come to fruition. Your plan should include a few contingencies that you have anticipated based on your knowledge and research of the coming situation. Your plans often need to be modified once you observe the situation "on the ground" (in the target area) and your contingency plans can be very helpful but, being flexible is key to being successful. You can waste a great deal of time spinning your wheels trying to attain your original goal when some slight modifications to your original plans/goals could result in a much more lucrative ending. Adapt to, and overcome, the hurdles in your way. Very rarely does "plowing through" the obstacles result in a desirable outcome. Assess what you observe once you're in the situation and be ready to think on your feet to take advantage of the unexpected opportunities presented to you, which is exactly what they are, unexpected opportunities that are there for you to exploit. Remember, the "enemy" has a vote, respect that fact and overcome that adversity.

Train Like You Fight

Probably the most important lesson I learned in the military was to train like I fight, i.e., conduct training as if I was in actual combat. Early in my career I didn't often do this. We would gloss over details stating, "if I were in combat I would do it this way" but that seldom works and actually causes you to develop "training scars." The more realistically you train, the better prepared you'll be for the fight. You never want to learn something new or figure out how to do something you blew off, in a "real world" situation. There will almost certainly be new things to deal with when you enter your real-world situation, and you must ensure the basic tasks are inherent. If the basics aren't second nature you will be dealing with unique situations with substandard skills. This means you'll be honing skills that should already be second nature while attempting to deal with an advanced threat. These actions usually result in failure. Hone the simple tasks to the point where you are using "muscle memory" for them so you can focus on the unknown tasks that require critical thinking. If you get bogged down with basic tasks that should be intuitive then you will lose focus on the bigger, more complex, tasks that require your full attention.

"Uniforms"

I used to not like the idea of wearing a uniform, it seemed restricting and conforming, which it totally was, but there is something to be said about not having to think about what you wear every day. It's liberating to be able to cut that part out of your life, one less thing you need to worry about. Since my retirement I have, somewhat, stuck to the uniform mentality. I have limited clothing and usually wear the same things on the same days. It's easier and, after all, who cares? My clothing is comfortable, nice, and functional. I could sit at a desk all day or get on a helicopter for a range tour. I wear the same shoes and have a spare set of "field" boots with a "go bag" at my desk.

When a piece of clothing wears out, I replace it. I have a summer set and a winter set of shirts. This makes it easier to get ready in the mornings and enables me to focus on the more important things in my life.

The "Acceptance" Double Standard

People are constantly trying to control others by telling them how to act or speak. Take combat warriors, for instance. Do you think that the Greeks told Spartans to be politically correct, or think about people's feelings, etc.? I seriously doubt it. I'm not saying that today's warriors should be mean or disparaging to others but, if a warrior is straightforward and honest, they shouldn't be condemned for it. Perhaps the people with whom the warrior speaks should grow stronger or accept the warrior for who they are like the warrior is expected to accept everyone else for who they are? There is an egregious double standard for those of us who have seen combat and returned feeling very differently after having seen the horrors of war and look at the world in a different way. As I said before, I was very lucky and saw very little of what you would call "combat".

I have engaged (not much) and been engaged (about the same) by the enemy but not nearly to the extent as some of my brothers who have experienced far worse than me. Regardless of one's experience, the fact remains that war changes a person and for others to take offense at the way a warrior acts is hypocritical. A warrior should be accepted just as everyone else is. Just as some request that a warrior attempt to understand others and adjust to appease others, those same "others" should do the same. But "others" should be aware that a warrior may not change their ways and that is ok. Warriors should be accepted for who they are, not shunned for being "offensive" or "abrasive". This should be acknowledged, and they should be accepted as fighters of wars. With this designation comes the most intense characteristics imaginable; characteristics that most will never understand but must accept.

Chapter 3

Parenting

While this section is called "Parenting" those without children should read it because you never know when you might find yourself in the care of a child, or someone who acts like a child, and this section can assist in those situations.

Parenting is a tricky subject because every single child is different. The differences may be minute and subtle, or overt and obvious, but they are there. Not all techniques work on all children but there are some things that have a universally positive effect that I think should be shared.

Structure

I'd say the most important thing in a child's life is structure. Keep them on a schedule. Wake up time, meals, naps, screen time, exercise time, outside time (if applicable), etc. should all be at the same time each day. We (are supposed to) keep our babies on a schedule but why do we stop when they get a little older? If you're unable to keep to a schedule naturally, use a tool to help, whether that be your phone, an alarm clock, calendar reminders, etc. and stick to it. Eventually you'll get into a groove and it'll just feel like it's time to do "X" thing. Eventually your child will help in some way by either crying, asking, or maybe just starting the next thing. If you need help with an example schedule just email me at jarrod@tryitlikethis.net.

Diligence and Sacrifice

The key to teaching your child anything is diligence and sacrifice. In order to form a stellar adult, you must have both. If you are lazy, give up too easily, or put your own desires first, your child simply won't learn as fast, if at all. If you consider your child an afterthought, or burden, then you don't really have to sacrifice anything, you can simply keep them alive and interact with them as you wish. The child will struggle at first (maybe their whole life), but you'll have your freedom and won't be burdened with having to care too much for the little human's future. On the other hand, if you truly want your child to become a great human someday, you must put in the work. You have to teach them constantly, and I don't just mean ABCs and 123s, I mean *everything*. Bear in mind that a majority of the teaching moments won't be on your timeline, they will occur when you least expect it – this is where the sacrifice comes in – as soon as you identify the teaching moment, drop what you're doing (within reason, keep your hands on the wheel, neutralize the charging bear, etc.) but try to capitalize on the moment as soon as possible because the moment is fleeting and your child may not learn the lesson as well, if at all, if you wait until the moment has passed.

Coddling

There seems to be a great deal of coddling of children, often for no constructive reason. If you coddle your child every time they are in distress they will never learn coping skills. This behavior is usually to serve the parent, not the child and, it can actually hurt the child worse than if the child had not been coddled. It makes a parent feel good to overprotect their child and they have trouble letting their child experience any adversity. I'm not suggesting you ignore them when they are experiencing that adversity but quickly assess the adversity and react accordingly. For instance, if your child sustains a minor injury, immediately assess the severity and provide the appropriate amount of care. If you supply a big hug and lollipop every time your child injures themselves, chances are your child will grow up expecting that kind of attention every time they experience even the slightest adversity. This train of thought doesn't just apply to physical injuries but also mental and/or emotional ones. Again, you must assess the level of adversity and provide the commensurate attention. All children are different and what worked for some may not work for your children and what worked for one of your children might not work for your other children. This measured reaction will prepare your children for adulthood. Sheltering your children from reality only prolongs the inevitable.

Becoming Obsolete

If you parent correctly you'll actually become extraneous to your kids, but you'll continue to parent and really annoy them. You will hear a lot of "I knows" and they will finish a great deal of your sentences. All of this is a good thing, it means your lessons have taken and your children are growing to be upstanding citizens. This is where you must back off on the menial instruction and focus on the big-ticket items, not that you have been neglecting the big-ticket items but now you can really dive deep on those subjects knowing that the basics have been covered. When I say "big ticket items" I mean finances, operating a motor vehicle, etc.

Honesty and Doing Their Best

There are many ways to successfully parent a child but two golden rules a child should know seem to be prevalent in all techniques: be honest and do your best.

<u>Honesty</u>

Teaching a child honesty, and the consequences of compromising that honesty, is an invaluable lesson that must always be reinforced. Reward honesty, punish dishonesty. Ensure the punishment fits the "crime," don't overdo it but don't ever let it slide. In addition to the punishment, explain to them why being dishonest is wrong. Tell them how it only takes one lie to violate trust and that violation is very difficult to overcome because you'll never know if they're telling the truth. The only way to truly make up for it is to tell the truth from that point forward. Once this lesson has been taught it is up to you to ensure that you are consistent. If they own up to doing something wrong you have to refrain from bringing down the hammer too harshly. Yes, there will be some circumstances where they will tell the truth and a punishment will be in order due to the nature of the offense, but you simply explain to them that the punishment would be much worse had they lied about it and you discovered the truth later. Again, fight the urge to punish too severely, recognize the courage it took to tell the truth and punish accordingly.

Doing their Best

By this I mean for them to always work hard and do their absolute best at whatever they do. This may be difficult but, if they try, then proper recognition is in order. They need to know that this applies to everything they do because, if they pick and choose when to give 100%, they may choose the wrong time and look foolish or lazy. They need to understand that teachers, employers, etc. look at the total person and expect that person to always perform well because, if they don't, the authority figure won't know when your kid will determine the task laid before them is unworthy of their best effort. Explain to them that while the job might not interest them, or they might not understand the purpose, to do their best because the reason behind the job will eventually be revealed and they will feel foolish or upset that they performed so poorly. This brings me to another reason they should always do their best…regret.

Regret

Most people can't foresee regret, either by choice or by ignorance. They minimize the feeling of regret to trick their mind into believing that doing a substandard job won't negatively affect them. Most realize, often after it's too late, that this is almost never the case. There are those who live in denial and attempt to quell the regret with lies of indifference, but the feeling is there. However, a feeling that is much more intense, and a significantly greater motivator, is the feeling of accomplishment.

Most of us have accomplished something in our lives that made us proud. It could have been a model you built when you were a kid, a promotion at work, or a project around the house but we've all had that feeling. It's a feeling designed to keep us motivated to do our best, to work hard and achieve something worthy of that feeling of accomplishment. If you explain this to your children and provide a small project that they can complete to feel the sense of accomplishment, it will help them understand and solidify that desire to do their best.

Educational Involvement

Speaking of "doing your best", one way to help your child do just that is to get involved with their education. I'm not talking about simply helping them with their homework (although that is extremely important) but really getting involved with their school – almost to the point of embarrassing them. Get to know their teachers, email them regularly if you have questions, subscribe to every school newsletter, sign up for email alerts with your child's grades, volunteer if able, get involved! The more involved you are with your child's education the more success they will have.

Bear in mind that education isn't just reading, writing, and arithmetic, it's teaching them all of that and everything else the school doesn't teach. Taxes, investing, sewing, survival, self-defense, self-confidence, etc. If you struggle with what they should know just search on the internet for "what should a ___ year old know?" and scroll through the results. Search "life lessons", life hacks, and/or life improvements and set aside some time every day or so to teach your kids these lessons. Teach them how to change a tire, shoot a gun, and start a fire. Teach them how to save their money, how to invest in real estate, and cook. Our job as parents is to flood our children with information so when they are on their own they have a leg up and can focus on important things like making money, having fun, and freedom. Parents often underestimate the learning abilities of their children. A child is a sponge from birth to five years old and can learn exponentially more than you think they can. Flood your child with information. Make every song, video, game, and toy an educational one. Don't waste a second of their formative years with any frivolity. Impossible, right? Not really. Did I do that with my kids? No way. I got lazy occasionally and let them watch some movies or TV shows that weren't exactly educational but, for the most part, I did stick to the "educational only" concept. People would say "you have to let them be kids too!" to which I say, how am I not? They do puzzles, and read books, and play with toys that challenge their motor skills, and teach them about shapes, colors, letters, and numbers...and they have a blast doing it! As a parent it is our job to endure songs, shows, and games that we do not necessarily enjoy so our child can prosper. I don't know of any parent who enjoys watching Barney, but kids love it, and they seem to be receptive. This is true of most children's activities, they aren't designed for us, they are designed for kids and kids love them. This isn't to say that you shouldn't expose them to advanced educational materials, as I said, children are capable of learning a great deal more than we think. You just have to spend the time on the correct things and not teaching them the hottest pop song or newest dance. While it is "cute" for a child to sing "Shake It Off" verbatim, it's not doing that much for their development. Maybe they should learn the alphabet, their numbers, and their shapes, first?

Real Time Education

All of this isn't to say you should do everything for your children. There is some benefit to what I call "real time education". If your children are having a hard time grasping the lessons you're teaching, they may have to experience the lesson themselves. Sometimes it's better to just let things happen instead of constantly trying to prevent your child from dealing with any adversity. You must decide based off some analysis of what will happen if the incident does occur and if the child will sustain an injury and the extent of that injury. If the results of the incident won't be catastrophic then you might want to let it happen. There really is no better lesson than experiencing something firsthand.

Make Your Children Better Than You

Regardless of the reason, I did not learn very many life lessons prior to starting my adult life and it was rough having to learn "the basics" while trying to figure out the military. I joined when I was seventeen years old and trying to figure out simple life lessons while also learning difficult military skills was challenging to say the least. Imagine having to learn basic social skills or balancing your budget while at the same time trying to learn how to navigate through a dense swamp at night or operate tactical radios. It was very tough to be behind everyone else socially and intellectually while still trying to keep up with training and I don't want my kids to have to go through that. I want my kids to know everything that I know and more. I want them to be exponentially better, smarter, and faster than I ever was. That's the goal after all, to make our kids better than us. Just think if every parent had that attitude. This world would be a far better place.

Unfortunately, there are many parents that feel that their children are a burden which never made sense to me, how can you blame a child for anything? You brought them into this world therefore it is your responsibility to shape them into an upstanding citizen. Children don't request to be born, they are brought into this world with nothing and need their parents to teach them everything. It's odd that I feel compelled to write that last sentence but, after working in child protection for two years, believe me when I say it definitely needs to be said.

Parenting Is Easy

Parenting, I've found, is one of the easiest, albeit challenging, jobs there is. I know, I know, some will scoff and say that I'm either doing it wrong or I'm lying but I'm serious. I don't understand why so many parents feel being a full-time parent is an arduous task as opposed to the blessing it truly is. It is amazing to have a first-hand effect on your children's life. To be there when they do all their "firsts", teaching them everything you possibly can, shaping them to be awesome. Who wouldn't want that "job"? You don't get a second chance at raising your children and we should all strive to do our very best as often as we can. If our best isn't good enough, we need to ask for help because we owe it to our children to provide them with the best chance of success possible. This is why it's so important for a child to have both parents involved in their life. I've been a single parent. It is a very challenging and selfless job, and I wouldn't have traded it for the world because it was what was best for my kids at the time, but I recognize that it would have been better with another parent who was as interested in raising my children correctly as I was. I've since married a wonderful woman who cares about my children as if they were her own and, for that, I am truly blessed. But this isn't the case for everyone, and some are left to do it on their own for most, if not all, of their children's life. While being a single parent is fulfilling it is also tough and not optimal for raising a child. A two-parent home with parents who love each other, or that at least don't fight in front of the children, is the best course of action but, having both parents involved in a child's life, regardless of the living arrangements, is exponentially better than only having one. Two parents who don't live in the same home but are amicable in front of the children are a suitable substitute for a two-parent home. I realize this isn't possible for many people but, if you're reading this and you don't have kids, wait, don't rush to have children. Ensure you are financially, physically, and emotionally secure prior to starting a family because raising kids is challenging enough, you don't need extra challenges making it even tougher. Like I say elsewhere in this book, a person's brain isn't even fully developed until the age of 25 (and I'm sure that varies with the individual) so wait on a family. Go to college, get a job, travel, etc. before you commit to having a child. A family is not something you want to force. It should feel "right", and you should be in the best possible situation to ensure you raise the child correctly.

Remember, your goal is to raise your child to be better than you, but you should also want them to speak highly of their childhood. It shouldn't be something they dread or something for which they need therapy. It should be an, for the most part, enjoyable experience filled with love and encouragement. Your child needs you, it can't live without you, and you can be as great of a parent as you want. Your upbringing, financial situation, and/or general lot in life does not matter when deciding how to raise your child. Love, attention, and information is what they crave and, if you can provide that, you will raise an upstanding citizen. If you're in a "cycle" of neglect, violence, etc., break that cycle. You have the power to do it. Simply decide that it stops with you and get on the right track.

Leaving the Nest

It seems odd to me that parents are so quick to get their children out of the house, and on their own, as soon as possible. Some parents speak of their children as a burden and have contempt for them when the reality is that the children did nothing to come into this world and actually have no responsibility to anyone. They were thrust into existence and should be provided everything they need for as long as they need it. It's a parent's job to love their children and prepare them for life such that the child will want to leave and be independent but not feel like they are obligated to leave. They shouldn't feel like they are not wanted because they are an encumbrance or impediment to their parent's happiness. I love my children and I am dreading the day they leave. I think of my children as my family, not little people for whom I'm responsible. This notion of "getting kids out of the house" is a relatively new idea. Families throughout history have traditionally stayed in the same home for generations and many cultures and families continue to do this. Not to say I want my kids to stay at home if they don't want to but how much more successful might some children be, as they transition into adulthood, if they were to spend the first couple of their adult years at "home". This would be an assist with not only expenses but advice for any unforeseen issues that may arise in their life. You could also be there to help with any life lessons that you may have overlooked or neglected to impart on them. Having this assistance as your child navigates adulthood is invaluable and could alleviate any roadblocks they may encounter. Some say this is a form of coddling and that doing this is not preparing their child to be on their own, but I disagree. I believe it is preparing them even more than if they were left to figure out all these new "basic" issues on their own. We as parents are obligated to tell our children everything we know so they don't have to learn this information on their own and are free to elevate to a higher plane of existence than us and learn even more than we know. When a child decides to venture out on their own they should be armed with all their parents' wisdom and the fact that their parents will always be there to help. This isn't to say you shouldn't let them make decisions or assist with solving their own issues but having a resource to help will give them a leg up on their peers and hopefully contribute to their success.

Using Their Advantage

Speaking of your children's peers, it is imperative that you stress to your children that while striving for greatness is important, they need not stress if they fall short of their goals. The fact that they are striving for that greatness puts them ahead of many of their peers anyway. Most of their peers are content with just getting by or being comfortable so, surpassing many of their peers will only require them to be slightly more ambitious. As their success is achieved they will become accustomed to achieving their goals and succeeding more often than those around them. While "beating" those around them is nowhere near the goal, it will assist in your child attaining what they want in life much faster. This will accelerate their success so they can secure financial freedom and peace of mind at a much younger age than you did which should be your goal. Setting children up for success is a parent's number one job, what they do with that preparation is up to them.

Parenting Is A Life Changing Event, Embrace It

Another thing I hear from parents is that their child is a drain on their personal life or that their child hinders their ability to do what they want to do and, to some extent, this is true. But a parent must change their mindset and accept the fact that they have a child now and that child is their responsibility. This is not to say that they can't do what they want, they may just have to be creative in the way they do it. This goes back to not fighting the plan but fighting the "enemy" I mentioned before. You may have to get creative or actually change your goals. I've often made the excuse that I can't workout like I want because I have children. I was mentally weak and used them as an excuse. I wanted to think that I wasn't in the shape I wanted because I had to look out for them and tend to their needs, but this was rarely the case. I simply made choices that precluded me from exercising or eating right. I could have packed more lunches/dinners or packed a bag with workout clothes so I could exercise while they were at their activities. Sometimes I did choose to pack lunches or have a gym bag in the car and, sometimes I actually used them, but other times I didn't use them at all. These were my choices, and I must live with the consequences. My point is, once you identify your shortfalls you empower yourself to overcome them. This requires a certain degree of self-awareness and presence to truly "force" yourself to do what's right for your future self. We often justify our actions without taking our future selves into consideration. One of the most popular justifications, or excuses, is that we should live in the now and do what makes us happy

right now. I submit to you that your behavior is only

creating the illusion of happiness when it is really based in

laziness or weakness. Doing the right thing actually brings

exponentially more happiness both in the present and the

future. Have the courage to do what's actually best for you

overall, not just in the moment. Having the strength and

discipline to achieve your goals while your children are

achieving theirs is a very important part of happiness.

Now, one caveat is that this technique is geared more

toward older kids of whom a parent isn't really supposed to

watch at practice. I fully support watching your "little one"

perform their ballet/soccer/t-ball activity. If you are in this

situation then you must be diligent about your diet and

work in exercise another way. For instance, I used to walk

around my middle daughter's baseball field (while pushing

my youngest daughter in the stroller) so I could get

exercise, entertain my youngest, and still watch my middle

daughter. Again, fight the enemy, not the plan, and get

creative! If you can't find the time to work out because you have children, then workout with your children. My toddler always wants to go for walks, but they don't walk like an adult, they play in puddles, pick up rocks, etc. This is not conducive to a good cardio workout but, you could wear a weight vest or a backpack with some weight in it or carry weights while you walk and lung/squat/do burpees while you wait for the puddle stomper. You must adapt and figure out a way to do it all successfully. Again, fight the enemy, not the plan.

Teaching Moments

As I stated earlier, take advantage of all teaching moments that come up in your child's life. Don't wait for the "perfect opportunity" to teach a lesson because it seldom happens. If you try to recreate the moment after it has passed, your child will not receive the full effect of the lesson and may not understand it at all. Taking the time to teach your child a lesson while in the moment will solidify

that lesson because they will have experienced it firsthand.
It may seem inopportune due to other things happening or
other people around, but a parent's first responsibility is to
their children. There will be those who scoff or disapprove
of you teaching your child a life lesson while in the
moment but simply disregard these people. As I said
before, free yourself from letting others affect your life,
especially when you're right. Also, if you are in the middle
of another task or activity, and it won't hinder anything too
much, stop what you're doing and take advantage of the
teaching moment. Parents need to stop worrying about
what others think, well, everyone needs to do this but
parents especially because not doing so could adversely
affect the development of your children. Bottom line, if
you feel like you should say something then say it, you may
not get another chance.

Pop Culture

When discussing entertainment with your child there is nothing wrong with explaining to them that it is perfectly fine to enjoy movies, television, music, sports, etc. without fully supporting the actual artist. I very rarely agree with the personal views of the artists' work I enjoy. It's seems like an odd thing to like something a great deal but not care for the creators of that content but, for me, it is quite common. I think that's what bonds us all though, the fact that we can all enjoy something regardless of what our views are. I enjoy listening to *Straight Outta Compton* because it sounds great, that doesn't mean I condone drive bys or hate the police. These "views" don't have to be simply social or political, they can be views on substance abuse, or the treatment of other people, etc. I believe this is why so many people take issue with artists expressing their opinions about world events. The artist's views aren't aligned with their own and they somehow think that the artist's opinion is worth less because they aren't an expert? But neither is the person complaining about the artist's views. Having said this, I think artists with large followings have a responsibility to remain neutral and limit their public opinions because they are not experts. These non-experts' followers sometimes consider their favorite artists to be experts based solely on their love for them and not any tangible evidence of the artists' expertise. So, be honest with your child about the true nature of the artist but also let them know that it's perfectly fine to enjoy an artist's work without blindly sharing their views or even liking them as a person at all.

Smoking Around Your Child

This next part could have gone in the "Observations" or Injustice" sections but I believe it belongs here because it is ultimately a parenting issue. The issue to which I'm referring is smoking in front of your kids and, more specifically, smoking while interacting with your kids. In the past smoking was "acceptable" due to the ignorance that surrounded it, but now that we know the inherent dangers, I think it is absolutely irresponsible for a parent to smoke around their children. I recently saw a parent with a cigarette between their fingers while they were helping their two-year-old catch a ball being thrown by their four-year-old sibling. I'm sure the parent justified this by being outside, but it was obvious that the child was ingesting secondhand smoke. Actually, there's no telling if the parent even cared that they were outside or if that child was ingesting their smoke. Most smokers justify secondhand smoke by stating that it is their right to smoke, the irony fully being lost that they are violating someone else's rights by exposing them to secondhand smoke. I wrote about this in the "injustice" section already so I'll stick to the point of the child abuse that occurs when a parent forces a child to ingest cigarette smoke. It really is amazing how society, more specifically government agencies, turn a blind eye to people that expose children to secondhand smoke. It's one thing to know the dangers of smoking and still do it to yourself but it is not right to negatively affect others, and a downright crime to affect children, especially your own. After much scrutiny I can only attribute it to weakness. A weakness that people disguise as exercising their personal freedom. But what about the freedom from illness to which a child is entitled? Some smokers don't think about that, they only focus on themselves and how it would be a hindrance to them if they had to stop smoking around their children or, heaven forbid, all together. I will also attribute this behavior to ignorance. From working in child protection, I have seen a great deal of ignorance regarding the care of a child. Now, maybe I was the ignorant, or naïve, one who believed the parents when they didn't know that beating a child, or fighting in front of a child, or smoking around a child is a detriment to them, but I don't think that is true for all the cases. Some of the people with whom I dealt seemed to truly not understand the dangers of secondhand smoke (or the other things I mentioned) because of how they were raised. They were never taught the correct way to parent. This is often the case with child protection investigations, the parents are simply doing what was done to them. This could all be alleviated by mandatory parenting classes but, that would be a violation of a person's rights, right? Probably. But I find it odd that you need a license to hunt, drive a car, fish, and get married but you don't need any prior qualifications to have a baby other than be fertile. Now, I wouldn't want anyone telling me if I could have a child or not so I don't condone this but, it seems like something should be done to better prepare people for the overwhelmingly important task of not just taking care of a human but ensuring that human is an upstanding member of society. But the most important injustice is that the child will do what they see their parents do, thereby increasing the chances that the child will smoke as well.

New Normal and Setting a Good Example

"New Normal" is a phrase some people use to prepare their children for changes in their lives. A death, a move, and/or a sudden change in financial status are sometimes described as the "new normal" or "new baseline" but I question those parents who wait for a catastrophe to adopt the "new normal" way of thinking. From the beginning I taught my kids the power and relief of acceptance. Accepting what has happened and moving forward. I didn't make a big deal about it, I didn't put a snappy name on it, I simply acted as though it was no big deal and that whatever is happening is happening and to accept it. This may seem callous and uncaring, but I submit that it is necessary in order to grow as a person. This isn't to say that I cheated my children out of pure emotion, on the contrary, if the situation warranted sadness or anger then of course they were encouraged to express it freely. But the emotion had to be commensurate with the incident. I know there are those who disagree with this line of thinking that if a child has an emotion then they should be able to express it and it is not anyone's place to tell them that their emotion is not valid or that they are overreacting. I disagree. We educate our children everything and controlling their emotions is no exception. I think there are limits that you must set as a parent to ensure that your child doesn't grow to become an emotional mess at the first sign of discomfort. As I mentioned elsewhere in this book, it is important in this life to be able to compartmentalize and normalize what's happening around you. For instance, my children rarely had an issue with going to a strange place like camp, or a new babysitter, etc. because I explained to them before they went that this is what's happening and it's a typical thing that kids do and that I would be available to them whenever they needed me, which I always ensured I was. If I was unable to be available, I told them so they could process that as well. There is nothing worse than telling your children you'll be there for them and then not being there for them. They must know that truth so they can cope with their situation better.

I've also had very little problems with new places. I think it was because I was never with one caregiver too long as a kid. I lived with my divorced mother who worked all day and I rarely saw my father before I was in high school. Honestly, I couldn't tell you the exact visitation plan, I'd have to ask my parents, but I do remember going to several different care givers, and I remember being on my own a lot, especially during the summer. I believe this helped when I joined the military because I never felt afraid or uneasy when I had to move to a new place, which I did often my first couple of years in the service. I just adopted the mindset that I owned the place and that I was supposed to be there. It really helped to adapt and settle into the new situation. When my kids experience a similar situation I tell them to adjust their mindset to feel like they've been there for years, and that it's not a new place/situation. This method will curb a lot of the anxiety allowing you to relax and enjoy the reason you're there, if it's supposed to be enjoyable (the POW camp in survival school wasn't all that enjoyable but adopting a confident attitude, like I was untouchable, helped me relax and focus on what I was supposed to do.) Worrying over what might happen is futile but mentally preparing for anything is productive. You don't even have to know what is coming, you just have to know that whatever it is, you're going to be calm, not freak out, and attack it with the same confidence and composure you'd have if you did know. Remember, your kids will react as you do, they look up to you and want to be you; set a good example as often as humanly possible because your kids will definitely remember every time you set a bad example.

Busy Kids

OK, gear change: if your children have activities after school (sports, a job, etc.) then you may want to reconsider them having to do chores at home. Yes, it is important for children to learn responsibility, but I submit that they already are by going to school all day, participating in their after-school activity, doing homework, playing music, etc. and it's not fair to them to have to do a lot of chores on top of all of that. They should keep their room clean, pick up after themselves, do their own laundry, etc., but having them do large, time consuming chores isn't the best idea when they already have limited time in the evenings.

Weekend chores are a different story. There's nothing wrong with having them tackle a larger chore on the weekend when they have more time. It's also a time to teach them how to do the larger chores that require more attention to detail than dishes or sweeping. A good technique, since they might not have much opportunity to make money, is to make a list of chores on the weekend. Put a money value next to each chore and let them decide who will do what. If one child is ambitious and knocks out a bunch, or all, of the chores then they have all learned a valuable lesson. Those who lean forward choose which chores they would like to do and, if the others slack off, the ambitious child may do all the chores and receive all the money.

Fathers

I have often been called "superdad" or "Mr. Mom" for doing things that parents are supposed to do. It really is sad that people, mostly females, feel the need to point out when a man is parenting correctly. It's not sad for them to say it, it's sad that they feel the need to say it because so few men are actually parenting. Our society has deemed it extraordinary when a man actually parents their children. What about all the mother's out there who don't parent correctly? They all seem to get a pass. I hear things like "they're doing their best" or "the husband doesn't help" etc. First of all, as I've already said, I've been a single parent and, while it's challenging, it's in no way impossible or even close to the hardest thing I've ever done. It's actually kinda easy if you're organized, selfless, and stick to a schedule (which is what children desperately need...structure.) Your children are a product of their raising and if you put in the work and raise them properly then you'll have very few issues. If you don't put in the work then you will suffer the consequences later and, at that point you must own the situation and attempt some damage control. No kids are "lost", and they all require your attention and love. If you put them first, you'll have very few issues. If you feel they are a "burden" or are "in the way" then being a parent will be extremely difficult.

I think fathers are doing more and more but there is still a stigma about doing a "mother's" job. A stigma that shouldn't exist and that I couldn't care less about. I never understood tough guys who can't change a diaper or feed a child or do anything that might bruise their delicate masculinity. Are their egos so fragile that they can't bear the thought of being seen having tea with their daughter? If I ever feel that way, which I rarely do, I simply think of my daughters and how much they want me to be there for them and any shred of doubt disappears. I absolutely can't wait to be there for my kids, they are the most important thing in my life, and they are my main focus, always. It's a pretty easy way to live, before I make any decision I evaluate the effect it will have on my children. If it will be a detriment to them, I don't do it. This isn't to say that all my decisions make my children happy, actually, more often than not the opposite is true. Our children think they want to be coddled, and given everything they ask for, but they actually seek structure and discipline and get weird if they are allowed to do something they know they shouldn't. This last statement hinges on your parenting technique. If you have parented properly, your children will recognize right from wrong and when they are misbehaving. Children may not choose the right thing all the time, but they will know that what they've done is wrong and act accordingly.

Priorities and Parenting Tips

You must decide to put your child first if you want them to be great. I feel that some people say they want what's best for their child, and they may, but they're not willing to put in the work so, do they really? It's not easy and it definitely isn't always fun but, you can minimize those "not fun" times by getting your mind right and know that this sacrifice is for a helpless child who needs your input, and selflessness, to succeed. It is vital that you put in the work with your kids, otherwise its shear chance if they pick up any useful life lessons, or anything at all. Well, they will definitely pick up what you do and imitate everything they see. This also has to do with diligence and perseverance. You must act as you want your children to, not as you want to (in front of them, anyway). If you struggle with listening to the same kid show over and over then invest in a tablet and let your child use their "TV time" with it at a low volume or in their room. You could also buy some wireless ear buds for about $8 and you use the tablet and let your child have the TV. You must get creative sometimes to stay diligent. Most of the time should be spent reading books, putting puzzles together, playing learning games on the tablet, etc. When they get to be about a year to 18 months old they are content with playing alone but you need to be there to direct them or help them when they hit a snag. Sit down at their level and talk through the game/activity. Teach them everything you can possibly think of because, after all, the goal is to make them better than you.

Knowledge Is Power

It's not just a saying, it's true. The more you know, the more you can do and the better chance of success you'll have. I tell my kids to never pass up a chance to learn. If they use the information, great, if not, now they know that information is not valuable. Either way they are learning. I also tell them to listen to everyone they encounter. Again, the information may be frivolous, or seem so at the time, but you never know what will happen in the future. Plus, listening is polite and, while the information may not be useful, the person may be in the future. Not in a sociopathic way but your child may encounter that person again and this time they may have something lucrative to tell/show them. They'll be glad they were polite and it's the right thing to do.

Meals

Another right thing to do is not force your children to "clean their plate" at meals. When I was a kid it was the norm, if the food was on your plate, you ate it. Parents used to use numerous reasons to get kids to clean their plate: starving kids, mom slaved over the meal, etc. but making a kid eat when they are not hungry is a bad idea for a couple of reasons. One reason is it teaches them bad eating habits that can lead to obesity. It took me years to get over the anxiety of throwing food away, I still struggle with it sometimes. Not to mention the fact that eating more than you should may lead to things like digestive issues, body weight struggles, etc. It will take some trial and error to find out how much to give your child and it will fluctuate often. Try your best to give them the correct portion but be fine with cutting them off if they've eaten enough and definitely don't force them to eat more than they want. Yes, of course there will be exceptions like when you introduce Brussels sprouts and your child claims that they are full when they really don't want to eat the sprouts. Make them at least try the sprouts and, next time maybe make something else for them to try. I firmly support making your child eat a variety of foods but some they just won't like (as there are foods we don't like) and continuing to serve your child foods you know they dislike makes for a contentious dinner time. What's the desired end state? If it's to torture your child then continue forcing them to eat the food they hate, if it's to ensure they are eating a healthy diet then find healthy things they like. I know that this is difficult if you didn't start early in their life but it's not impossible. You may have to find different ways to prepare the foods they dislike or use a healthy condiment, etc. That being said, yes, there are starving kids elsewhere who would love that food but forcing your child to eat when they are full is not going to help them. If this is truly your goal, send money to a charity or volunteer at a soup kitchen.

Family Dinners

Once their old enough, it's perfectly fine for children to make their own meals. The idea of sitting down as a family for dinner can be difficult, and often impossible, due to conflicting schedules, homework, etc. This isn't to say that you shouldn't ever have "family dinners" on occasion when it's convenient as to not hinder each other's progress. It may not happen every day, most times you'll have to see each family member one on one or a couple at a time and there's nothing wrong with that. The bad thing is forcing a "bonding" session when other things loom over your heads. When your kids are involved in after school activities they may not be home until late and it's a terrible idea to eat a huge meal so close to bedtime anyway. They usually have time to come home, fix themselves a sensible, nutritious dinner, do their homework, play music, and then hang out a little until it's time for bed. We get to spend time together during homework help, or when they're eating or before bed. It doesn't seem like enough, but I know the other activities are important also. Plus, as children get older, they want to spend less and less time with their parents, not out of any spite or angst, although that does occur, but more out of wanting to talk to their friends, have alone time, etc. You definitely get to spend considerably more time with your children while their young, cherish it.

Selflessness and Volunteerism

Speaking of soup kitchens, I think a valuable lesson the children of this country aren't being taught is selflessness and volunteerism. My daughters and I used to volunteer at the local homeless shelter making/serving lunch and then cleaning the kitchen afterward. After several weeks of this the girls understood the value of helping others and it became second nature to them. If you make volunteering and selflessness a way of life for your children, it will be that much easier for them to do. If they think of it as a normal thing, and understand the good they are doing, then they will be more apt to do charitable things on their own and continue to do them in the future.

Financial Lessons for kids

Denying your children things they want simply to "teach them a lesson" about doing without is not optimal. That being said, you should teach them the difference between needs and wants and explain to them that you are there for their needs and will attempt to supply their wants. This isn't to say that they shouldn't be thankful for the things they need, that should be a lesson taught very early in their life. Ensuring they say please and thank you will assist them in the future when dealing with others. You should also tell your children if you can't afford something and that you will save your money to buy that item. It doesn't illustrate your incompetence, on the contrary, it shows them that you have a budget to which you adhere and that you will purchase their item when the budget allows. If it's something they want, you can also suggest that they save their allowance to buy the item. You should be paying your child an allowance that is both commensurate with their age and your salary. If you make a small amount of money then the allowance should be an amount that won't stress the family budget but, if you have the money, you should increase the amount they receive. Along with that allowance must come financial education.

Teach your children to split their money into four groups: saving, spending, investing, and charity. Fully explain these categories and ensure they adhere to those lessons. Don't let them use their savings to buy things they want, that's the spending section. Investing will mean something different for each age group but you can explain to younger investors that you will invest their money for them and show them how you do it, explain it down to a level they will comprehend (based on their level of understanding), not necessarily their age due to children developing differently. It's a good idea to instill in your children a desire to give as well. If they get into a habit of donating to charity it will last for their entire life. Have a discussion about to which charity they would like to give and then donate together so they can feel what it's like to give. Follow up by showing them how their money is being used and who it is helping so they understand why charity is important.

Parenting Techniques

I don't understand those videos/pics I see on the internet of children doing things like covering themselves in peanut butter or painting a motorcycle. Where were their parents?! It's crazy to me that children of that age are left alone in an area where they have access to those types of things. I'm a firm believer of "child proofing" one's house. It's unrealistic to think you'll be able to have eyes on your child every second, it's nearly impossible and not conducive to a sane lifestyle. However, there is a limit to the length and nature of the lapse in supervision and certain measures must be implemented in order to ensure your child's safety. Leaving your child in an area where they have access to items that can cause permanent damage to themselves, others, or your property is borderline child neglect, and sometimes crosses that threshold. You must do an honest assessment of the area in which your child operates. If you do not want them to leave the area, put up a gate. If they will be left alone in an area with hazards (which should be in case of an emergency only) use a camera to keep an eye on them. But, most of all you and your children should be in the same area where you are actively engaged with them or so close that only a glance will update you on their wellbeing. Yes, this seems tedious to some but it's what's required of a parent. Tedium is one of the necessary "evils" of being a parent so embrace that fact and choose to enjoy it or you will be miserable. Whatever you choose, please don't ignore your children, enjoy every second you have with them because they won't be around your house for the majority of their life and you need to soak up as much time with them as you can.

Bottom Line

I've covered a couple of different issues in this section but if you don't remember anything else, remember this: if you want your kid to do something, you must do it. If you don't want your kid to do something, don't do it (in front of them, anyway.) A single action is worth a thousand lectures and is significantly more impactful on a child. They watch you every second and emulate you. I realize it's tough sometimes, and we do our best not to make any catastrophic errors, but we also have to let ourselves off the hook if we have a few "missteps". The best way to prevent these kinds of blunders is to always strive to focus on what's important, your children's wellbeing and healthy growth. They need you to be your best so they can be their best.

Chapter 4

Observations

"Legal" Age?

It's odd how society sticks with decisions made for reasons that don't really apply anymore or aren't totally sound given what we know about child development. 18 to vote, 21 to drink, 25 to rent a car. 25 to rent a car comes from statistics, collisions decrease significantly as people reach the age of 25. I believe this is due to the development of their prefrontal cortex which I go into more later. The 26th amendment gives us our right to vote at 18 because if you are old enough to be drafted you should be old enough to vote on why you're being drafted. But there isn't a draft anymore so should we still have this rule? Is a person developed enough to do either? It depends on the individual and their maturity and level of self-awareness.

What about kids who go to college and live off their parents for another four to eight years? Are they less mature than those who join the military or enter the work force at 18? What about kids who do both? This is assuming all people are the same which couldn't be farther from the truth. So how do they justify it? It's too hard to scrutinize each individual so they lump everyone together and deal with the fallout. I've met 18-year-old kids that could be astronauts and I've met some who should still be under constant supervision (myself being a perfect example of the latter – thank you military!). I think the better option would be to assess each kid and determine their level of maturity. Should some 18-year-olds be denied the right to vote due to their lack of cognitive ability? Maybe. How much cognitive ability should an 18-year-old have? Should they have to pass a simple civics exam before they vote? Should they be required to take a computer-based class on each candidate before they vote? People wouldn't stand for it, "I'm 18, by God, and I have the right to vote!" It doesn't make sense. I'm not talking about voter suppression; I'm simply talking about common sense. If you have no idea who the candidates are, let alone for what they stand, how can you make an informed decision at the ballot box? But America is about freedom, not necessarily logic.

What about 21 being the legal drinking/smoking age? Yes, kids get in less accidents if you don't let them drink until they're 21 but kids are also 4 years away from having the full ability to properly reason. There are some people who are older than 25 who still don't have the ability to reason adequately. Maybe some of them suffered prefrontal cortex damage from the alcohol and weed they consumed prior to turning 25? Maybe it delayed their development? I know many youths may balk at this notion, but I believe we put entirely too much emphasis on drinking and drugs. People can't wait to take their child to a bar on their 21st birthday like it's some important milestone to have your first drink (although it's rarely someone's first drink due to alcohol and drugs being so glamorized in this country. I had my first drink well before I turned 21). What is this saying to those children? That alcohol is now an important part of your life? That it is a "normal" thing you should do now that you're old enough to do it? The legal smoking age is 21, should they start smoking as well?

It really is crazy how much emphasis we (the U.S.) put on drinking, especially given how detrimental it is to a developing brain. As I said, a 21-year-old kid is four years away from having a fully developed pre-frontal cortex yet "we" encourage them to drink alcohol, a substance known to decrease cognitive function, cause memory issues, and result in brain atrophy. This is not setting your child up for success.

Individuality

It doesn't make any sense to me that people care about what others think of them regarding their outward appearance, so much so that they spend exorbitant amounts of money to uphold the appearance, regardless of how much it will set them back financially. Now, I'm not talking about being a slob. There is something to be said about presenting as pleasing an appearance as possible to ensure you are able to achieve your goals and not burn bridges but following trends simply because others say you should is weak. There was a similar issue when I was in the military, often functionality lost out to dress and appearance standards. It didn't matter that it was raining, snowing, or extremely hot, you must adhere to the standard – common sense will not be tolerated! I think they have, somewhat, gotten away from that mentality, but not completely. More fields should adopt the functionality over "fashion" idea, I'm sure productivity would increase significantly. Back to those who feel they have to buy the hottest clothes or follow the latest trends - they seem like slaves or lemmings. Doing what others say simply because they deem it "cool" or "hip"? It just doesn't make sense and seems very disingenuous and maybe a little shallow. What difference does it make? It must be exhausting to have to keep up with what others deem is "trendy". I don't see the point.

Language

Profanity is defined as "blasphemous or obscene language". Blasphemous or obscene by whose standards? Who decides that a sound is profane? What about words that are not "profane" but mean something far worse than those deemed as "profanity"? It's asinine that a harmless sound can be determined to be a "bad" word. This is a completely antiquated way of thinking. Our society has progressed some in this regard. Television allows far more "bad" words than they used to, and certain words have become accepted in polite conversation. But there are still those who judge others by their words and feel that using profanity is lazy or uncivilized. But it's about the context of your word, not the word itself. If I use a "profane" word in a completely innocuous way, how can it be "profane?" If I'm simply making a sound with my mouth that is not designed to offend, how can it be offensive? Yet there are those words and phrases that are used to actually disparage others but are perfectly acceptable to say in public. This makes no sense. Just think how much more we would progress if we weren't hung up on little things like what words a person uses. People are so easily offended. Some wear it as a badge of honor and can't wait to be offended so they can get on their self-righteous high horse and condemn the offender. Their frail sensibilities are such that the slightest utterance that disturbs their fragile emotional state is absolutely unbearable. But most of those who feign offense are simply being disingenuous and only saying they're offended because they dislike the person using the "profane" language or they're attempting to make themselves look better for political or social reasons. For those who are truly offended by what someone says, grow up and grow stronger, mentally. I don't understand how a person can allow another person to negatively affect them with words, especially if they know the "offensive" person is intentionally trying to be offensive? When you adopt this mentality you become untouchable. Nothing will bother you because you will have ascended to a higher plane of existence. A world where words don't have power over you, but you have ultimate power over them – you either disregard what the offender is saying because it is untrue and not worthy of a response or you use the offensive speak as a catalyst to improve yourself. Either way you are in control.

Nerd Wars

"Nerds." What does that mean exactly? There are people who give other people a hard time because they know everything about a certain subject like Star Wars, Star Trek, or Dungeons and Dragons but, what about those who study and memorize sports statistics? These people are just as nerdy. Seriously, what's the difference between a cos player and a sports fan who wears sports jerseys, caps, etc.? Bear in mind I'm not saying that either thing is bad, I think everyone has things in which their interested and there's nothing wrong with any of it. It's all a waste of time and money and I think about this every time I buy a sports team onesie, t-shirt, or go to a ball game. It's inexplicable how we can justify spending way too much money on crap that has our favorite movie, sports team, or TV show on it. What are we trying to say? Do we want everyone to know we love that thing? Are we seeking attention? Do we secretly want the actors/players to see us? I honestly have no idea why I spend money on these things other than I enjoy them and that's what life is all about, being happy.

There seems to be some disparity regarding what is acceptable to know way too much about and what isn't. Times are changing but there are still remnants of people who condemn those who know a great deal about "nerdery" like Dungeons and Dragons, Magic the Gathering, comic books, etc. yet these same people can quote every single sports stat and watch shows that discuss sports ad nauseam. Some people also can't understand how a person can watch another person play a video game, yet those same people will sit down and watch a sporting event for three hours. How are these two things different? The truth is that they aren't, we all have things that we enjoy and none of them are any better or worse than anything else. I used to be VERY opinionated, some would say I still am (this book?) but I have grown up a lot and realized that, for things that don't really matter, everyone is entitled to their opinion.

It's amazing how we can feel so strongly about something when we're young and then come to a realization about that subject and can't believe we ever thought that way. I know people older than me, and much smarter than me, who still hold on to the antiquated notion that if a person doesn't live exactly how they live then that person is wrong. This way of thinking is based on culture, whether it be a career, religion, ethnicity, etc., and it is very hard to overcome, especially when you still adhere to the viewpoints and rules of that influence.

Mental Maturity

We all, inexplicably, make mistakes and dumb decisions in our lives. I say inexplicably because there are many times when we behave in a manner that we know to be detrimental to us yet continue to do it. The key is to grow as a human, ascend to a higher mental plane, and help ourselves by not doing the dumb stuff. People reach that point at different times in their lives while some never reach it. If you're a parent, you must strive to reach that point as soon as possible so you can properly prepare your children. The sooner you reach your mental maturity the sooner you'll be able to pass on that lesson to your children. This will empower them to reach their mental maturity level even sooner than you did. This will also make your children's life better and help the world by having smarter, more responsible people running the place. If you don't have children, it is your responsibility to achieve as high a level of mental maturity as possible so you can live the best life you can. When I say "mental maturity" I only mean not making life decisions that are detrimental to you and those around you. There is absolutely nothing wrong with having fun, being silly, etc., in fact it's essential to retain this characteristic whether you have children or not. I always find it funny when people take themselves too seriously and act as if having fun or being goofy is somehow only for children.

Fights/Assault

Fights. I touch on this in the "People Are Still Doing That" section but an observation I had was why do people fight? Is it in their nature? Are they just naturally angry? Bullies? Do they love the challenge of a fight? I'm not talking about self-defense but initiating a fight for no good reason. Some fight because they don't like what someone has said to them, as if fighting that person will somehow change reality. What I mean is, if someone says something disparaging to you, fighting them won't change the truth, whatever truth that may be. They're either saying it to you to get a rise out of you or it is actually true. Either way, fighting them won't change anything and it could possibly result in you getting injured, them getting injured or both of you ending up in jail. It's hilarious when "tough" guys get pissed over someone talking smack to them. It shows their weakness. Truly "tough" guys don't listen to those who they can destroy and/or are only trying to get under their skin. Weak people lose control and get upset over words. The same can be said about those guys who beat women. Regardless of what they say/do, short of trying to murder you or your family, there's nothing women can say or do that should result in them getting beaten. That is the ultimate weakness. I get it though, I can understand how a weak person may lose control, obviously it happens often, but someone who has ascended to a higher plane of existence understands that if that person is being so mean or inappropriate that you feel you want to hit them then you shouldn't be around that person. Even if they are sweet and nice sometimes, how do you know which is the true them? You must cut ties and find someone who wouldn't dream of talking to you like that but not out of fear but because they love you too much.

Thin Skin

I never understood people who get upset at insults. If the insult is true, and it's something you can control, then there's nothing else to say. If the insult is regarding something you can't control or isn't true, there is still nothing else to say. Why would anyone get upset about something they can't control or that isn't true? It's true weakness to allow another person to affect your mood when it is blatantly clear that that is their goal. You empower that person. Instead, try either ignoring that person or respond with a polite comment. The main thing is to stay calm and not let it bother you. I don't mean act like it doesn't bother you on the outside and still wrestle with it internally, but actually not let it bother you. The truly tough people I've met in my life were very unlikely to fight over something someone said. They couldn't be bothered by the weaker person because they knew that it wasn't worth their effort. It may seem difficult, but it can be very easy. Once you switch your mind to adopt this technique, you won't be able to do anything else in the future. It really is liberating to legitimately not care what people say when they are trying to get under your skin.

When I say this I'm not talking about constructive criticism that can actually help you grow as a person, this advice should definitely be heard and heeded. Even if the criticism is said in a mean way or intended to hurt your feelings, truth is truth. If someone identifies something about you that is a detriment to your personal growth, you need to be honest with yourself and correct your actions…or don't and continue to suffer the consequences of that negative behavior. Getting upset and/or fighting someone over something they said won't change anything. If what they said is not true, who cares? If you choose to fight someone over something they said, you are even weaker than before because you allow others to control your actions. Truly strong people do not let weak people control them. It may feel good to lash out or throw an annoying jerk an "a**-whoopin'" but, it isn't optimal, because it's too easy for it to escalate. It's much easier, and more satisfying, to ignore the offender and not give them the satisfaction they're seeking.

The U.S.

Speaking of strength, some people don't believe that The United States is the best country in the world. They base this view on statistics, graphs, government, etc. But, when people say that The U.S. is the best they aren't talking about stats or leaders, they're talking about how one has the freedom to do virtually anything they want in this country. This country is not defined by its corrupt and/or weak leaders but by its opportunity. People who say America is the best are talking about how this country is comprised of a diverse array of cultures and people and how that diversity makes this country great. I really don't think that regular citizens of other countries understand the sheer magnitude and density of the U.S. I've spoken to a number of foreign nationals who lay out their travel plans for when they visit the U.S., and some have consisted of visiting Florida, New York, Texas, California, and Seattle all within the same week. While this is technically doable, it's certainly not easy and you certainly wouldn't be able to fully experience each state. It makes me wonder if this mentality is prevalent in most countries. I'm sure most of the citizens of the world are able to read a map or use the internet to determine the vastness of the U.S. but I still don't think people understand until they actually visit.

The possibilities and opportunities in the U.S. are endless and, usually, the only thing stopping a person from achieving their goals is themselves. I couldn't imagine living anywhere else. I'm sure I would get used to it, but I would miss the absolute freedom of living in the U.S. I always wonder why people speak ill of the U.S. yet millions of people from all over the world come here seeking a better life. I also wonder why those who claim to hate it stay, and those who threaten to leave it never do? I believe it's because everyone is well aware of how great it is here. The people who make these threats are angry at the leaders of our country (depending on who is in office at any given time although I've never heard a conservative person threaten to leave the country when a liberal politician is elected to office). You can't judge an entire country on the behavior of its government. Frankly, there are many people who condemn those who speak ill of China or Iran stating that it's the governments of those countries, not the people, who are causing the problems yet, when asked about the U.S. they say the country is in peril or the country is horrible. Why isn't the U.S. afforded the same considerations as other countries? The fact is, regardless of who is in power, the U.S. marches on and continues to be great. People speak of the violence and compare us to other countries without even realizing that most of the countries to which we are compared are barely the size of one of our states. The sheer immensity of our country and the fact that we have 50 very unique states is what makes us great. I've been all over the world and I've enjoyed many foreign countries, but I would never trade the freedom I enjoy in the U.S. to live anywhere else.

Science

I find it hilarious when scientists describe naturally

occurring phenomena like it's some sort of magic or

miracle. I was listening to a scientist on a podcast and he

was talking about how some pipes are designed to prevent

water from freezing because the pipe is too strong and

won't let the water freeze because of its force and that it

just keeps pushing back against the water to prevent it from

freezing. It's a fact, it was designed by humans, yet he was

saying it like it was some sort of black magic, getting very

animated and dramatic. It seemed very silly and fake.

Things happen. Once you observe them happening then

that's it, it's no longer odd or crazy, it just is. Calm down.

Also, if someone sees something for the first time it doesn't

mean they discovered it. People were watching things

falling from trees long before Isaac Newton was hit on the

head but, because he wrote it down, he "discovered" it. If

you truly invent something then I can see getting some

credit – and I'm not talking about a theory, theories are just guesses, or assumptions of something, not fact. People base a lot of "facts" on theories. "Well, according to this theory, this is true." It's fine until they make documentaries, or kid shows, based on these unproven theories. No one knows for sure what the dinosaurs looked like. There are many theories, but no one is absolutely sure yet there are countless dinosaur books/shows/etc. about what they did and how they acted, etc. Not "they may have" but "they did". It seems irresponsible the number of theories that are touted as fact. The most egregious one, in my opinion, is the big bang. How anyone can definitively say they know how the universe started, or was created, etc. is preposterous. There is absolutely no way to know for sure. They also say the universe is expanding because of the light shift to the red end of the spectrum but how do they know for sure that indicates expansion? Which way is it going and from where is it expanding? I thought it was infinite? I'm sure some big brain can explain it all to me using theories and assumptions, but I think these same big

brains feel the need to control something that is

uncontrollable, and unfathomable. The answer of "man, I

have no idea" is not in their vocabulary. They feel

everything can be explained if you stick to a theory. Well,

who's to say the theories are correct? We just blindly

follow these theories as if they are fact but who cares,

right? No one can prove them wrong, well, not yet anyway

and by the time someone does we'll all be long gone so,

again, who cares? "We" (humans) used to think we were

the center of the solar system. Imagine what humans will

know a thousand years from now. We'll probably look like

cavemen to them. But again, I digress. We were

discussing how giddy scientists get when they observe

natural phenomena. If something occurs and you see it

then that's it, its nature doing its thing. No need to get all

crazy about it, it's just the way things are. Now, if it

happens once in a blue moon then I could see getting

excited about it. How often? Why so seldom? Etc. But

this excitement over a natural occurrence feels disingenuous. As I alluded to earlier, 1000 years ago "scientists" had it all figured out and then the scientists who came after them scoffed at their ignorance and provided their own explanations, theories, etc. Then those who came after that generation did the same and so on. It would be interesting to see what we got wrong and what we got right.

This isn't to say all science is bull or that all scientists are full of it, I'm only talking about those who rely heavily on theory rather than fact. Science is absolutely necessary, and I actually don't think we spend enough money and time on science. I wonder how many issues could be solved if people actually cared about science? Or the right science? Why would anyone waste their time on experiments that don't directly help humanity, or the Earth, etc.? There are many frivolous experiments that waste precious funding on nonsensical tests. I guess it has a lot to do with money and who is funding these experiments, and how the request for that money was written and what is done with the money, and how closely those two resemble each other. But know that years from now we will be laughed at or condemned for what we are doing today.

Being Helpful

Since when is it weak to expeditiously help someone? Is this just an anomaly that I have encountered or is this an actual issue? What I mean is, when someone asks certain people for help, or they task them with something, those people don't act in a timely manner. Instead, they take their time and drag out the process until the absolute last minute because they feel if they act with efficiency and vigor then they are a chump who is being manipulated by "the man". They mock those who react immediately to a task to complete that task as soon as possible. I never understood putting off a task if you don't have to. Why wouldn't you want to get that done and out of the way so you can be ready for the next thing? The more you procrastinate the more the work accumulates. It's also very liberating to complete a task, it gives you a sense of accomplishment that is just as good as any drug. I think people take issue with acting this way because they feel like they're doing it for someone else so, who cares? But the way I look at it, once I am tasked with something, I own it, it's mine, and I am going to crush it as quickly and professionally as I can. There is nothing wrong with leaning forward and knocking out work. Yes, usually your good deeds will be "punished" by more work but revel in the extra work, know that you are excelling while the others are left behind and use that momentum to rise through the "ranks".

"Heroes"

It's crazy to me that people see athletes, movie
stars, etc., as their heroes. Why are these people singled
out and made famous? I could see if they really did
something heroic, but the real heroes are the cops, fireman,
medical professionals, and military members who put their
lives on the line every day. Why aren't there trading cards
for actual heroes? Why aren't there more books about
actual heroes? They won't sell? Who's to say? We'd
rather invest money in professional athletes and actors.
Why don't we pay the real heroes a salary that is
commensurate with their job importance? Because those
who make the rules don't care about real heroes, they only
care about using those people until they can't use them
anymore. Yes, they get an adequate paycheck, "good"
benefits (debatable, why isn't all their healthcare free like
the military?), and a retirement. Some government
retirements were very substantial, but those times are

ending. It was too much for those in charge to reward our heroes and those heroes aren't actively doing anything for those in charge once they retire so there is no longer a need to take care of them. That's the nature of life, use resources until they are depleted and then move onto the next resource. It's actually sadder than that. I believe it's just people being people. You can never account for how an individual person will act or react. If you get the "right" person in charge then real change can be accomplished but, in government, the "right" person seldom rises through the ranks because you can make considerably more money in the private sector. It's almost like we need people who are already financially secure to be in charge of government agencies. This would alleviate the need for selfish decisions. Similarly, if only the "right" people would seek public office we wouldn't have to worry about them immediately seeking reelection the minute they were elected and they would actually focus on fixing the issues of this country, but this is for another section. So, we will continue to look at athletes, celebrities, etc. as heroes and pay excessive amounts of money for them to entertain us (yes, sports are entertainment, it's not anything meaningful, it's the same as going to the movies or watching TV.) while real heroes barely get by and get treated like they owe us or, even worse, that they are the enemy.

Integrity

Why do so many people have issues with the truth or, at least being genuine? It seems like people watch what they say so they don't give too much away or try to hide something to bring up later. People spend so much time trying to hide their true intentions or true feelings that they don't move forward in their life. They're so concerned with looking weak or being embarrassed that they often hesitate to say what they really mean. Other people don't say what they mean or expose their true intentions because they are trying to manipulate people into doing their will or thinking a certain way. People have a hard time figuring out how to take me if they don't know me because I speak from the heart and tell people exactly what I think. I don't try to sugarcoat anything or alter the truth to suit the situation. Some people may think this makes me naïve or gullible, but I've achieved a great deal being this way. I think people appreciate honesty and, frankly, it's exhausting to be any other way than honest. Some people spend so much time in their life trying to manipulate others instead of just speaking their mind and getting things done that are mutually beneficial to all involved.

Living

I never understood why people care about how other people live their life if it doesn't directly affect them. Like the phrase "he's wasting his life "or "she's not doing anything productive in her life" doesn't really make sense especially given the fact we don't really know why we're here (in this life), or what we're supposed to be doing, or if it even matters. But those of us who do want to do productive things with our lives and who want to do our best shouldn't be hindered by those who don't, or anybody else for that matter. The one constant, the one absolute truth in this life, is that no one has the right to adversely affect anybody else. If they do, or if they think they can, the person they are adversely affecting should have every right to stop and/or prevent that person from doing it ever again. I often talk about how we'll never live in a utopian society. We're so far from it now that it doesn't even make sense when people talk about it. By utopian I mean a world where everyone is taken care of, everyone always has enough food, water, shelter, no one is better than anyone else, etc. But the people that tote this ideal are either being willfully ignorant or are incredibly naïve. Most people that pitch this idea are politicians, just vote for them and they'll provide everything you need! But have they? Can they? Who determines what you need? It should be you, right? But if you allow someone else to provide for you then you must live by their definitions and their rules. In addition to "knowledge is power" I also tell my children that money is freedom. Having it allows you to live how you want. Not having it makes you a slave. A slave to bills, a slave to the government, a slave to your employer, etc. The whole point of America is that you can do whatever you want here. There are no rules against a person being successful. The government tries to deter success through taxes, regulations, etc. but it can still be achieved despite these roadblocks. This way of life gives people hope. If you take away that dream of success, then people just become sheep and are forced to live a certain way with no hope of ascension. In addition to these aforementioned facts, even if most people agreed to live in a utopian society, they fail to take into consideration the "wild cards", people who, no matter how great a situation is, will screw everything up for everyone. Selfish people, sociopaths, mentally ill, etc. There are people who are either only looking out for themselves and really don't care about everyone else or people who can't help the way they are and are overtaken by some kind of psychosis to the point that living harmoniously with other humans is too challenging. These people will never be happy in a utopian society because they will always want more than the other guy or disregard the other guy and act selfishly. What about religious zealots who bastardize their adopted religion into one of hate and use that "justification" to hurt others? As you can see, there are many variables that make a harmonious society impossible. The best thing you can do is to ensure you are happy, make as much money as possible while also helping your fellow humans. Now, if everyone adopted this model, we'd be in a lot better shape as a society.

Best Intentions

In the same vein as an idealistic society, most corrupted things started with the best intentions. Congress, unions, welfare, etc. all started out as necessary programs to help the people of this country. We needed a government and, while I'm not so naïve to think that when congress was formed it wasn't full of rich white guys, I do believe that they formed that body with the best intentions and did a lot of good for the country in the beginning. But, like everything run by the elite, it always grows the wrong way and has now become a place of liars, dullards, and ne'er-do-wells. People who are only looking out for themselves while they grandstand on TV on the house/senate floor, lying about trying to help us.

Unions seem to have gone down the same path. At first, they were absolutely necessary to ensure workers were paid a fair wage and not abused or killed on the job. But now, from my personal experience, they have become a shield against actual complaints from an employer. I've seen employees stay employed even though their work is shoddy to the point where everyone in the office knows but nothing can be done because the employee is part of a union. It's not fair to the rest of the employees who work hard and do a good job.

Another program that has seem to have deteriorated is welfare. A great idea, if used correctly unfortunately, it has become what I fear it was ultimately designed to do, keep Americans dependent on the government to justify the government. I firmly believe that we should be giving people a hand up, not a handout. Too often people rely on welfare money and can't find a reason to do anything else, and why should they? Some people are perfectly content with doing nothing and getting paid for it. There should be limits to the support and whoever issues that support should work diligently to help the receiver out of their situation. Unfortunately, the government runs welfare and, just like everything else the government runs, it is inefficient and undermanned. Well, I say undermanned but knowing what I know about government agencies, they are rife with lazy people who take advantage of the regulations against firing employees (mostly due to unions). So, the actual workers are overworked, the lazy workers don't do anything, and some people on welfare continue to exploit the system.

Obviously not everyone on welfare is lazy or cheating the system but there are enough that it is causing a drain on our governments funds which are supplied by those of us who are not on welfare. There needs to be stipulations for receiving welfare. For instance, before a person receives money from the government, money they are not entitled to but receive due to the benevolence of the government, they should be drug tested to ensure they are not spending money on unnecessary things. They should also receive classes on budgeting, parenting (if applicable), job searching, etc. Basically, they should attend classes on everything that will help them successfully get off of welfare.

Phone Use

Why are people so concerned with other people being on their phone so much? This is a new age and is not the same as it was before phones. How do you know what those people are doing on their phones when you criticize or scoff at them? Maybe they're talking to a family member, or working, or shopping for a gift for someone. How many people do you converse with now that you have a smart phone vs. when you didn't? This may not even apply to most reading this since smart phones have been around for so long. There was a time when you went days without interacting with loved ones or friends. You would either have to call to "catch up" or speak to them in person. Having a smart phone allows us to connect with whomever, whenever via text, email, or social media. For some of us who live far away from our friends and family, it's a nice way to keep up with what's going on in their lives without having wait so long between long "catch up" phone calls. Very few of us have the time to sit on the phone for hours "touching base" with all our family/friends. Being able to scroll through multiple people's feeds to get an update or at least feel connected is invaluable to those of us who barely see our friends and family. So, cut us a break, we're not always just goofing off.

Driving

Most of us do it and some a great deal. It seems we're all different people behind the wheel, some more aggressive, some more cautious. Often these two personalities clash on the road. Some people are too aggressive, some are simply wanting to get to point B without being held up by those who are not very concerned with getting anywhere in a timely manner. Sometimes a person who is in a hurry or drives with a purpose will come up behind someone and inadvertently "tailgate" that person. Usually it's not malicious, they are simply letting the person in front of them know that they are behind them and would like to get by. This especially happens when the slower person is in the passing lane (in the U.S. this is the left lane) and the faster person is trying to get by them. The only logical explanation for the slow driver in the fast lane is ignorance which then turns to belligerence when the faster person comes up behind them. The slower person must not know the rule and then take offense when the faster person expects them to move over. That's a real issue in the U.S., the belligerence of those who are doing the wrong thing. I'll never understand it. A person drives incorrectly, another driver honks or tailgates or shoots them a look and then the driver in the wrong becomes angry (and probably gives them the finger.) In the instance of tailgating, I've heard people brag that they intentionally slow down to annoy the driver behind them even more. They are in the wrong and then do something to "punish" the innocent driver who is simply trying to get where they are going in a timely manner. People wonder why we don't live in a utopian society; this is one of the reasons. I'm actually the opposite. If I find myself "cruising" in the left lane, not paying attention, and I see someone in my rearview mirror trying to get by, I can't get over fast enough. I actually feel bad for doing the wrong thing. What a concept, taking responsibility for my actions and having remorse and then correcting the situation humbly and expeditiously. Those who intentionally hinder another's progress by not letting them merge or slow down and not get over so a person can pass are usually people who claim to be nice and considerate otherwise and think they are doing the world a favor by not allowing someone to pass and/or merge. It's crazy. How can you consider yourself a nice person when you are intentionally doing something to annoy someone else? The reality is, you're the jerk. I'm simply suggesting, don't be? I see a lot of Facebook posts about how people slow down when someone is tailgating them or not letting people merge if they don't feel the merging is "correct", or any other countless unfriendly driving techniques. It seems like the people who do the abovementioned unfriendly acts feel like they are more important than everybody else. How else do they justify intentionally driving slowly or blocking the lane or not letting others merge? Are they teaching the other person a "lesson"? How arrogant, and mean, to try to control someone else simply because you feel you're "right". The person who is trying to get to where they're going isn't trying to bother anyone, they're just driving expeditiously. Unfortunately, there are those who take this type of driving personally and intentionally impede another driver which is extremely petty. As I said, the disturbing thing is that people who brag about impeding others also claim to be the nicest people and that they care about others yet have no issue acting in this manner. If they were nice, they would yield to the person behind them, or the person trying to merge, etc.

I mentioned it before, but I really can't believe people are still cruising in the left lane. I get it, it very well could be due to ignorance of the law which brings up a great point, what happened to driver's education being mandatory in high school?!! I grew up in Illinois where you took a full semester of classroom and a full semester of behind the wheel. I think a lot of the issues people have on the road could be alleviated by implementing this model throughout the country. In some places you pay between

$550 and $800 to take a driver's education class, the same

class that was included in my high school education. Is it

any wonder why some people drive the way they do? I

can't imagine the situation on the road getting any better if

people aren't mandated to take a formal driver's education

course. It seems very irresponsible of state and federal

governments to allow untrained drivers on the road.

Chapter 5

People Are Still Doing That?

There are a ton of things people do that boggle the mind, things we know to have no positive benefit to our lives and are often actually a detriment. Why do we do these things? Habit? Weakness? Defiance? Probably a combination of all of these and more. It really is amazing that we will intentionally do something that we know we will suffer for later. I understand this behavior in young people, (I did a bunch of dumb things when I was younger that I can't explain) but as we grow older, we're supposed to grow smarter (or, at least have more knowledge) and not make the same mistakes we did in the past. Nevertheless, there are countless people who continually make the same "mistakes" and pay for them exponentially each time. People often say "I don't know why I did that" but we all know why we do things, because we want to. It's very disingenuous for us to lie and say we don't know why we did something. We should own the fact that we knew what we were doing. There is no mysterious force controlling us, there is only us and our desire to do what we want. The way to ascend is to own what we do and learn from it. We can either disregard the feelings we have urging us against making the same mistake, and suffer the same consequences, or learn from the "mistake" and strive to not give in to our weaknesses.

Smoking

In the past, cigarettes and cigars made people stink, stained fingers and teeth, covered everything in a disgusting film, etc. But I could possibly understand smoking back then when people had no idea cigarettes/cigars/etc. were a detriment to one's health, especially when the tobacco companies were telling people that, if they smoke, they will be cool, or get girls/guys, etc.,

I kinda get it. However, now that we know smoking is responsible for almost half a million deaths a year (over 40k due to secondhand smoke – a subject we'll cover shortly), I don't get it at all. What's the attraction? Is the buzz that good that people MUST have it? Is the constant rise in price worth it? That's another issue I don't get, people keep paying more and more for something that is a detriment to them. I used to smoke for a long time, from high school until a little less than halfway through my military career. Then, one day I came to my senses and quit cold turkey. I realized how ridiculous it was and just quit. I hear people say they are "addicted" but that is just one of two things: 1) They're weak or 2) They don't want to quit. I think the latter is the hardest because, although people know they shouldn't smoke, some simply don't want to quit, and it is nearly impossible to stop doing something if you don't want to. Those in the first category know who they are. They are too weak to endure the cravings and/or the withdrawals. This is the epitome of weakness and is very shortsighted. People allow their cravings and withdrawal side effects to control their lives when they should be in control of their own life. If you want to quit, simply decide that you are not going to let anything control you and that you don't "need" anything that isn't going to help you be a better version of you.

Drugs

Speaking of drugs (which is what nicotine is), I can't believe people still do them. I've never done any hard drugs, just smoked some pot in high school, but I have consumed my fair share of alcohol and taken prescription drugs on orders from a doctor and I'm sure the experience is similar. In the not-so-distant past I had an epiphany. I'm the type of person who boils things down to the root issue and tries to decide why something is done and I simply can't understand being under the influence of anything anymore. The thought of not being in control or leaving my behavior to chance is no longer a risk I'm willing to take. Regarding alcohol, one of the most harmful drugs, there is the argument of only having one or two a night, but I don't see the point of that either, I mean, what is the purpose? Some say to wind down, some lie to themselves and say it's for their heart, others say it helps them sleep but there have been numerous studies that debunk most of that. As far as alcohol (specifically red wine) being "healthy", the jury is still out, most of the web sites I've seen on the subject use "may" and "assumption" liberally and never actually commit to the idea that red wine is "good" for you. It really is odd that people adamantly justify alcohol when it is the same if not worse than some illegal drugs regarding the pain it causes its users. Why is it legal and all other drugs aren't? Heroin used to be prescribed by doctors and I don't remember anything in the history books about an opioid epidemic. Heck, they used to put cocaine in soft drinks, did this result in everyone developing a cocaine habit? It really does seem odd that a drug like alcohol, given all the damage it causes humans, is legal but almost everything else isn't.

If you think about it there is no logical reason for anything a person chooses to ingest to be illegal. People say that some drugs make people do things that are illegal but so does alcohol. People say that some drugs make you violent. So does alcohol, in some people. The only reason I can really think of is that it has become a societal norm and that it's a huge business. Those two factors usually justify anything. As far as drugs "making" someone do something illegal, that's another reason not to do them but that's not a justification to make drugs illegal.

Speaking of drugs that are "good" for you, marijuana has become mainstream now due to its "harmless" nature. Weed advocates insist that it's far more harmless than alcohol which may be true, to a point. I haven't found any definitive studies stating that children under 25 are less susceptible to brain damage by smoking pot than they are from drinking alcohol. Yes, I said "children" under 25 because a person's prefrontal cortex isn't fully developed until they're 25 or so. That means that all those children (myself included) who were drinking massive amounts of alcohol, and those smoking weed and doing other drugs, were crushing the part of the brain responsible for rational thought before it was fully capable of rational thought. This begs the question, if someone waited until their prefrontal cortex was fully developed before they made the decision to use drugs/alcohol, would they do it at all? I doubt it. I would venture to say that people drink alcohol/use drugs because they were brought up in a culture that celebrated it. Parents and other adults around me drank, and looked like they were having fun, so kids then thought it was cool and they did it. I was brought up to think drinking was the norm and that if you didn't drink you were weird or lame. How many of my dendrites were damaged I wonder? Looking back, I think I had a lot of fun, but I often wonder what would have happened if I would have refrained and focused on important things? Or simply refrained in order to give my brain a chance to fully form?

Daylight Savings Time

Daylight savings time. Just when you and/or your kids get on a schedule they shift us an hour and everyone gets jacked up. Is anyone really benefiting from it anymore? If so, tough, most of us aren't and we shouldn't be catering to the few, the few should be conforming to the masses. This can be said about a great deal of other things too.

Street Fighting

Something else I don't understand is street fighting. I totally get MMA, Jiu-Jitsu, etc., they're great ways to stay in shape, hone skills to defend yourself against criminals, and satisfy a natural desire for competition and combat. But, getting in fights as an adult? I don't understand it. Let me preface this by saying that I've had my share of bar/street/etc. fights and I'm very lucky that I didn't hurt someone, get hurt, or wind up in jail. That's the problem with "illegal" fights, you just don't know how they're going to end, and that uncertainty is not how someone who has ascended behaves. Obviously I'm not talking about defense (self, family, friends, and innocent victims), I'm talking about fighting for no good reason. Why are they even fighting? I touched on this in the observations section. It seems like some people just like to do it, it's like a contest or test of manhood but these people don't account for the terrible things that could happen, or maybe they just don't care? Either way, fighting is a risky proposition and shouldn't be conducted impulsively.

Bike Safety

I can only chalk up this next part to ignorance but how are people still riding their bikes against the flow of traffic and walking with the flow of traffic? Parents, for the love of God, please teach your children to walk against traffic and ride their bikes with traffic. They're going to get hurt someday and it'll be unnecessary. Shoot, teach them bike safety in general: helmets, hand/arm signals, etc. It's not enough to ensure they can walk/ride, you must include every aspect of every task you teach them. Leaving anything out is setting them up for failure. The only explanation is that the parents don't know either? It's not only dangerous but a real pain in the butt. I'm that guy who "on the spot corrects" kids when they're doing either one of these things. They always look at me with either contempt or fear but at least the word is getting out.

Speaking of bicycle safety, I can't believe people are still using those child bike seats that attach to the bike itself – what happens if the bike falls over, or you run into something, etc.? It seems like the child would be very susceptible to injury if the bike were to fall on its side? I suggest the trailer because the child can sit comfortably and you can put some toys, books, etc. in there in case they get bored. If they're strapped into the seat on the bike they just have to sit there. Also, with the trailer, if the bike falls on its side it won't harm the child because the mechanism that attaches the trailer to the bike isn't rigid and allows for the bike to fall while keeping the trailer upright. Some will say the bike seat is cheaper, but I don't think sacrificing safety for frugality is prudent – also, a quick internet search shows that most seats are comparable in price to a trailer.

Trends/Fads

Trends or Fads. I never really understood this concept. A person or persons think that something is "cool" so other people do it? Like wearing the same kind of clothes, or "costumes" as I call them. I don't understand why anyone would want to look like someone else. Even when I was "following" trends I never really understood why I was doing it. I felt weird like I was trying to be someone I wasn't. I think as little kids we all do it, we just want to be like our buddies and do what they do but, as we got older, we started doing things that strangers do simply to be "cool". I grew up in the 70s and 80s (1970s and 80s that is) and a trend I only tried a couple times was putting a tight roll in the bottom of my jeans. I never thought it looked "cool" and I thought it looked feminine and dumb for guys. I felt weird doing it and stopped immediately. I believe after that is when I stopped following trends/fads, or at least I stopped following the popular ones. I think I based my "look" off those who didn't follow the norm and bucked the system. I guess that's another way of following a trend/fad, even though it's only trendy to a certain group of people. I never tried to be anyone else, I don't think. I just tried to be comfortable and not look like everyone else. I think the fact that we were poor and that I already had crappy clothes helped immensely. It's not hard to look like a rebel (read: dirtbag) when you don't have any other choice. I did have a couple sets of "nice" clothes, but they weren't "name brand" so they weren't really "nice" in anyone's eyes. I used to get asked by "cool" people where I got my clothes and I would just say "the mall" even though I really had no idea where they came from because my parents/family bought them for me (this is probably why I loathe shopping). The cool people would ask in what store in the mall I bought my clothing in an obvious attempt to shame me into lying or admitting that the clothes came from Walmart or K-mart. Truthfully, I did know that they didn't come from the mall but I didn't really want to deal with any crap from them. These events, coupled with the fact that I spent most of my life in the military, probably formed my negative opinion of fads or being trendy. It just seems fake and contrived, like people are trying to be someone they aren't to try to impress people who they shouldn't care about anyway. If someone is judging you on where you buy your clothes or what type of shirts you wear then the issue is with them, not you. You can look every bit as "presentable" with cheap clothing as you can with expensive clothing. Actually, the people that buy expensive clothing simply for the fashion value of it are chumps who waste their money on things that don't matter. Now, that's not to say that "expensive" clothes are always bad. Sometimes buying an expensive coat or shirt is important so it will last, whereas a "cheap" coat or shirt may not be very well made and may wear out prematurely. But you may not have the option to buy the expensive thing, you may only be able to buy the "cheap" thing more frequently due to your financial situation, and there's nothing wrong with that – as long as you are being frugal to work toward increasing your success and your mental growth. The bottom line is to be yourself, be comfortable, and not worry about the opinions of those who don't matter. For those whose opinions do matter (employer, spouse, etc.) ensure you are presentable and, most importantly, let your performance define you, not your fashion.

Triggers

Wow, it appears the people I've mentioned so far "trigger" me? Not really. Have I triggered you? How many triggers do you have? I love how the psychology world (or whoever) take a perfectly decent word like trigger and use it for their own psychobabble. Oh, you heard a song or saw an image that you didn't like or that reminded you of a traumatic time in your life? No kidding, it happens to all of us. But now it has a name and is trendy, and trendy people use it, and now we can censor people or put up "trigger warnings" so we don't make anyone remember anything or feel anxiety, etc. This is called life. It is not everyone else's responsibility to ensure that you go through life being warned before you encounter adversity. It is your job to grow stronger so when you are faced with these "triggers" you can control yourself and deal with the resulting emotions in a manner equal to the strength you know you have. Yes, sometimes we hear things that shock us or remind us of something horrible but, it's our job to arm ourselves with logic and mental strength in order to prevent being overwhelmed by things that happened in the past, make us upset, or disturb us. Some say that people should watch what they say so they don't make others feel bad but, as I've said, no one can make you feel bad, you can only allow others to negatively affect you. We empower people to negatively affect us because they are unable to do so without our consent.

Jealousy

Along these same lines is the feeling of jealousy. I never understood how someone could be jealous of someone else but not try to better themselves to reach, or surpass, the level of whom they are jealous. If you're jealous of someone and you don't do anything about it then you're just a whiner who wants things handed to them. When I look at someone successful, who has worked hard to get what they have, I don't aspire to be them, per se, but

I do admire them and evaluate/emulate their techniques so that I can be as successful as them, if not more so.

Everyone learns something from somewhere and it's usually from another person. Utilize all your resources to get ahead. This also reminds me of people who say things like "do you think you're better than me?" or "that guy thinks he's better than everyone else" which makes no sense. Better at what? Soccer, making money, chess, etc.? It's a desperate cry from someone with low, or no, self-esteem. I don't understand why anyone would care what anyone else thinks, especially someone they don't admire or respect. It gets back to jealousy. Don't be jealous or envious, just strive to have the best that everyone else has while being happy for them for having it because that's what this country is all about: Life, Liberty, and the Pursuit of Happiness. I think a lot of people have forgotten about that last part.

"Judging"

I also don't understand the phrase "if you don't know my story then don't judge me." First of all, who is judging you? Usually people who say this either care the most about what people think or have some hang up with their past. These people are quick to tell people not to judge them because the strife they've endured is so horrible that it somehow justifies their current actions. This is BS. Nothing justifies poor behavior. I have had my share of hardships, as have other fine, upstanding citizens, and we don't feel the need to live a substandard or questionable lifestyle then justify it by saying our past was rough. To truly ascend you must learn from your past, extract every nugget of useful information, every lesson, and then discard the waste. Use the goodness to ascend and be happy.

Seeking Recognition

What is the obsession with getting recognition for the things we do? I could understand if you are constantly putting out effort and are continually treated poorly or continually getting passed over for a well-deserved promotion but if you are doing good works for others then the fact that those others are receiving help should be enough. No one should seek out recognition or praise for the things they do because it makes the original act seem disingenuous. If you truly care about helping others, the thought of thanks never crosses your mind. Only those whose goal is to receive validation or commendation request acclaim for their "good" works. I've run into this situation a couple times in the military where a person feels they deserve recognition, and they will actually highlight themselves for the things they have accomplished. This praise and recognition would naturally occur when they turn in their after-action review or provide bullet statements for their evaluation, but some people ensure everyone knows how well they did and it makes them look as though they only did it for the recognition, not the country.

In everyday life, the deed, and subsequent joy the recipient receives, should be thanks enough. Actually, given this rationale, every good work is a tad selfish because of the feeling one gets when they perform a kind gesture or an "unselfish" act. That good feeling should be enough. This is what it's all about, putting the other guy/event/cause first. Men and women should join the military to serve and the feeling of pride that comes with knowing you've served your country, and protected those in your unit, should be enough to satisfy any desire for recognition. This is what I loved most about "special operations", the fact that very few people even knew what we did yet we had such a significant effect on the mission. BL: do "good" works because they need to be done, not to get recognition.

Chapter 6

Injustice

Active School Shooters

This next part is a serious issue that most schools in this country aren't dealing with properly. I'm speaking about active shooters and the very minimum effort being exerted to prevent them. Most of the schools in my children's district still leave their front doors unlocked, although my child's middle school has decided this year to lock the door, which is promising. Instead, most spend thousands of dollars to hire a company who teaches administrators how to conduct active shooter drills. These active shooter drills are conducted poorly and don't really train the children to react appropriately. My daughter came home from school one day, visibly upset, stating that they had conducted an active shooter drill but, due to poor execution of the drill she was scared that she still didn't

know what to do if an active shooter should come into the

building. I have explained to her many times what she

should do (run, hide, fight) but, as I mentioned before, if

you don't "train like you fight" you won't be prepared for

the battle. My daughter's class just talked about what they

would do but didn't conduct the actual drill. Since I teach

my daughters to assess every situation, and ask questions if

something doesn't make sense, my daughter made her

assessment. Based on that assessment, and the fact that her

classroom was on the second floor, she asked her teacher if

the school could purchase portable fire escape ladders so

she and her classmates could go out the window and climb

down to safety. Her teacher said no and that the school

wouldn't spend money on things like that. It was

absolutely gut wrenching to see my daughter so distraught

over not feeling ready to execute and trying to do

something about it and still being shut down. If she were to

actually practice an active shooter drill on a regular basis it would become second nature or "muscle memory".

Instead, she lives every day with the anxiety that something might happen. I've asked our school district about this and they are worried that an actual active shooter drill will scare the children but, what about a real situation? I think the fear will be exponentially worse if a real situation arises and the children aren't properly trained. Training (practice) instills confidence and reduces fear. If the children were to train properly, they would still be fearful but confident in their ability. This confidence, coupled with muscle memory, would allow them to act and most likely save lives. Schools can't just go through the motions, especially when dealing with life threatening situations like an active shooter. The drills need to be accurate and often. The children must do and say everything they will do in an actual active shooter situation otherwise they will develop training scars that could get them or their classmates hurt or killed. I truly believe that, since active shooter situations happen so seldom, that some school districts develop a false sense of security and "play the odds", hoping it never happens to them. I'm sure the school administrators of Parkland, Sandy Hook, and Columbine thought the same. If I see a threat I do everything I can to eliminate, or at least mitigate, it and sometimes that mitigation requires the help of someone else (like a school district). It's extremely frustrating, and frightening, when they won't act. A school's number one job is to protect its students and schools all over this country are failing at this task. They mainly fail due to poor leadership and mismanagement of allotted funds.

Secondhand smoke

If there's one thing in life that I absolutely abhor, its injustice. I'm not talking about bad luck; I mean when someone's actions negatively affect someone else. For instance, as I mentioned before, secondhand smoke - the fact that a person has no issue forcing those around them to inhale something that is a detriment to them is the very embodiment of injustice. The argument is "what? I'm outside!" as if being outside somehow makes the smoke harmless. But it stands to reason that a person who is intentionally causing themselves harm wouldn't care about harming others. This secondhand smoke issue also applies to marijuana. As I've said several times in this book, I couldn't care less what you do with your body, put whatever you want into it but don't force me to ingest it. Now that marijuana is legal in Alaska every idiot is out on the street toking up. They're doing it in their cars, on sidewalks, in front of stores, and at children's baseball games. Legalizing it has caused people to be emboldened because, even if they are caught in these places (which is almost impossible unless a cop happens to be walking by at that time) the punishment is so insignificant that the risk is worth it. So, because there aren't enough people available, or willing, to put an end to it, it continues. I'm open to "retaliation" suggestions – maybe a spray bottle?

Human Roadblocks

Another injustice in this world are inherently lazy people who are gatekeepers to your goals. There will always be those people who just want to coast or "play the long game" and not expedite your process because they don't want to move on to the next project, if there is one. When I worked at Air Force Special Operations Command, I often heard the phrase "this is a marathon, not a sprint, son" from some of the civilians who worked there. Unfortunately, the warfighter doesn't have time to wait for a "marathon", they need help immediately. Fortunately for those on the front lines, everyone has a boss, and the bosses of these particular civilians were active-duty officers whose responsibility was to the warfighter so, I only needed to tell them the truth about the situation to get an expedited result. The most frustrating thing is that the people who are going to be a roadblock to you can often do all this leg work themselves, they simply don't want to. You must be willing to do the leg work for your effort.

Speaking of getting things done, motivated people are often hindered by those who want to control their little piece of the world instead of doing what they can to help their "customer". When I encounter someone who refuses to do their job, or says "no" instead of finding a way to "yes" I ask them what would happen if warfighters did that, what if we gave excuses, or took an exorbitant amount of time to act, etc.? People would die and America would lose its freedom. They don't like that because it convicts them of their complacency and intentional hindrance of progress. This is another reason why we will never have a utopian society because there are those who focus more on themselves than others. Hoping for this paradise is so very futile and a colossal waste of time. This isn't to say that you or I shouldn't help others, but we must also hold others accountable and insist that they act when their actions are essential to our success. Often "gatekeepers" will become upset with you for "going around" them but you mustn't let this dissuade you from acting. Simply document all your efforts to achieve these goals the "right" way to show that you attempted the "normal" procedures and that they clearly don't work. I put "right" in quotes because the only reason it is the "right" way is because the "gatekeepers" have deemed it so. The gatekeepers love to tell you to "trust the process" even though the process is inefficient and often broken. There is always another way to solve a problem, don't be afraid to find another solution and present it to the "gatekeeper's" boss, ensuring that you explain why you had to go outside of "normal" channels to ensure the next guy doesn't have to endure this arduous procedure in the future. Remember, document everything, no matter how inconsequential it may seem at the time. This will give you "ammunition" when asked about your deviation from "the process".

"Progressive" Techniques in Schools

As I stated elsewhere, I don't believe "touchy-feely" or "progressive" seminars and/or community interaction will help with issues. I'm speaking mainly of voluntary meetings with students to stop school violence/bullying, etc. I believe the people who attend these things are already on board and there is no guarantee that you'll reach the people who actually need the help. Schools have assemblies and conferences that are not mandatory and they expect to reach the problem kids. They waste money and time on techniques that do not guarantee results. Even if the target audience does attend there is no assurance that they will be receptive to the information. Instead, it's just an exercise in futility. As I stated previously, anti-bullying seminars and half-hearted active shooter drills are perfect examples of these techniques. Having resource officers, conducting "hands on" or "live" training, and locking school front doors are the way to combat threats. Hoping you can talk a bully or active shooter out of their behavior should be done after all tangible safety precautions have been implemented.

Chapter 7

The US Education System

Since we're talking about the education system in this country, I'd like to address some glaring shortfalls. The education system in this country is run by the administrators who make their decisions based on what they think is right instead of what kids actually need. There is an exorbitant amount of fraud, waste, and abuse of taxpayer money within the education system. They spend money on trendy social programs and flash in the pan educational methods (like commercialized personalized learning) instead of tangible things that the districts need. It's laughable that the administrators think that teachers are so incompetent that they need to spend millions of dollars on companies to implement personalized learning – a technique that every educator is well aware of and the good ones practice daily. How arrogant for these administrators to think that educators need their help to do their job when the money can be spent on countless other concrete necessities.

Grades

Another aspect of the education system that makes little sense when you boil it down are grades. What is the purpose of grades other than to impress some college sometime in the future with how much you retained? What if you don't go to college? Why not have a pass/fail system? My father taught high school for thirty years and he once told me that the whole grading system was a sham. His idea was that you stay in the same grade until you can accomplish the tasks at that level. If you can read, do math, etc. at that corresponding grade level then you move up to the next. If you can't then you stick around until you can perform those tasks. I have spoken to many educators about this idea and they all spew the same garbage about how it's more of a detriment to the student if they are held back than if they move to the next grade without attaining all of the required knowledge of the last. The educators I spoke to are obviously talking socially, not realistically, and they definitely aren't looking out for the student or the next grade's teacher either. The student moves up not knowing how to read at that level and then must receive special treatment from the teacher because they are unable to learn the new material since they never learned the material from the previous grade. The education system pays a lot of lip service but truly couldn't care less about students. If they did, they would keep kids in the same grade until they passed all the requirements to move to the next grade. Some reading this will say "they did meet those requirements" meaning that they did well enough to move up but not well enough to function at the next grade level. It really is sad that those students who struggle are destined to struggle for the rest of their school career and beyond. But none of what I propose is politically correct so the educational meat grinder will continue to squeeze out kids who are ill prepared for the world because those who can make change (administrators) are too busy either trying to make themselves look good or are too weak to do what's necessary. How do you combat this? As I said in the Parenting chapter about parental involvement in school, parents must be involved with their child's education or they leave their child's success to chance…and the chances are not good.

Physical Education

Why isn't there more Physical Education in schools? When I was in school we had PE every day. It's no wonder why there is an obesity problem in this country. "Our" children aren't set up for success by being taught how to live a healthy lifestyle or, at least forced to get some exercise each day.

Educational Stagnation

Having a teenager who is adamant about her education gives me insight on our current school construct. It's as if our education system simply teaches what they always have because that's the way it's always been done. This is rarely a good reason to do anything. Our children should be spending most of their day learning lessons that will help them be awesome humans instead of lessons that they may never use again. For some of the population I believe advanced algebra, calculus, trigonometry, geometric proofs, etc. are important to their work but, for most of us, it is never used. I'm on the fence about some of the basic math concepts too. For instance, I can't remember a time when I needed to use graph paper to find an x and y axis, or relied on estimating to find an answer to anything (mainly due to the fact that an estimate is not at all accurate and I will eventually have to figure out the exact answer.

I've also never used polynomials, or quadratic equations or point slope. Instead of cramming a ton of potentially useless information into our children's day, why not focus on the basics and take some extra time to ensure that they actually understand it. This would cut down on the need for homework which would allow for our kids to do extracurricular activities after school and not have to worry about getting homework done. A typical evening for my kids is to go to swim practice for two hours (this often doesn't include changing, showering, etc.) then coming home to grab some dinner, then homework, music (if they didn't do it in the morning), then bed. This leaves them little time to decompress and relax from the day. Yes, I could take them out of swimming which would free up a significant chunk of time in the evenings but when would they do physical training? Elementary schools only have P.E. once or twice a week and it's not always an adequate workout. As I said before, it's no wonder why there is an obesity epidemic in this country, we don't value exercise and health as much as we do other things. I touch on healthcare elsewhere in the book but, it would cost significantly less if people were healthier. So, I will continue to have my children involved in some type of physical activity every day and, since they both love swimming, that's what they do. But this still leaves the issue that the U.S. Education system is not maximizing my children's potential. My high school age daughter is constantly texting me stating that she is bored and that she is wasting her time at school. She says that there is too much down time and she is not being challenged. I understand that this might not be the case for every student, but I would bet that it's true for more than we think. Some classes pile on the irrelevant work while others have too much down time, but students can't work on homework from another class in their less intensive classes so they just have to sit and waste their time resulting in less free time later. Time is a huge factor that people gloss over. It's the one thing that we can't get back yet schools (among other entities) waste it like we have plenty.

The bottom line is that school should be pass/fail. If a child can show that they have learned the information for that grade level, they can then move on to the next. On the other hand, if a student is struggling with the information, they either stay behind or take extra classes (summer/night/etc.) until they do understand the information. The only reason the education system is this way is because those in charge of it have made it that way. Just like the legal system, the education system has become bastardized to the point where it serves those working for it more than for whom the system was created. If the education system truly cared about the students, and not those who worked within the system, things would change immediately. But this isn't the case. Those in the system work disproportionately for themselves (or the unions work for those who work in the system) to perpetuate the issues that have been prevalent for decades, if not centuries.

Teachers are the obvious exception as they are the ones grinding it out in the classrooms doing the work. Granted, some are doing more than others but it seems like most of them, from my experience, work very hard to help our kids.

In the education system, money is constantly being misspent, as is the case with most government entities. They are self-licking ice cream cones that are designed to serve themselves first and their people a distant second and their "customers" a distant, and sometimes non-existent" last. Those in administrative positions, at least the ones I've experienced, are out of touch with the schools and what is actually needed. They would rather give other administrators raises, or waste money on frivolous programs of which there is no way to prove their worth and are only implemented to make the administrator seem like they are doing something constructive. This has always been the problem with hierarchies like these. As I mentioned before, those at the top very rarely have their fingers on the pulse of what's happening on the "front line." Why do they need to put in the work to find out the real issues plaguing their districts? They've been there and done that (20 years ago) and don't need any rookie teacher (less than 10 years) telling them what they need. Most administrators, leaders, etc. are simply looking for the best way to get them recognition, promotion, etc. and they do very little to mask those ambitions. The problem is that, unless they do something illegal, they are virtually untouchable. All of that to say this: If you have the money/time/inclination, home school your children. If you have the money but not the time, send your kids to private school. While most of the teachers my children have had were phenomenal, they are also hamstrung by those above them and are unable to fully perform as they'd like. Homeschooling seems like the only logical solution. Personalized attention, no wasted time, ability to deep dive on a subject if desired, time to branch out to other subjects like finances, driving, etc. The structure and rules of a public school are not conducive to making a child great, only adequate. It is up to the parents to supplement the mediocre (usually no fault of the teachers) education their children receive in order to properly prepare them for the future. Especially those people in low-income areas whose schools don't receive as much funding as other schools. It is not only necessary but imperative for a parent(s) to supplement the education their child receives from the public school system. You do have a choice as a parent. Don't be a victim.

Chapter 8

Quick Hits

- The definition of accomplishment is something you've done, not what you will do. Don't let what you've done define you. Keep striving for more and better achievements. Goals are huge until they become accomplishments. Don't focus on the accomplishments, strive to achieve more goals.

- If you're struggling with your weight, eat a little less and move a little more. Contact me for advice: jarrod@tryitlikethis.net. Find creative ways to get moving. For instance, if your only option is to walk but it's too easy, find hills, wear a weight vest, and/or hold something in your hands to tone upper body muscles. Work with what you have; use your imagination.

- When sending emails or saving files, be descriptive with your names to ease finding the information later using the "search" function.

- If you find yourself struggling to complete a task, large or small, significant or minute, I believe it is your subconscious trying to stop or correct you. If this happens, stop and reevaluate the situation. You're probably trying to tell yourself to attack this from different angle or foregoing it completely. Either way, don't keep forcing it.

- Don't always assume that your kids or spouse know what you are thinking – tell them you love them, tell them you miss them, tell them you're proud of them, and hug them often.

- Question: is it better to enjoy the music or lyrics of a song? Can a song be good if the lyrics aren't? Vice versa? I rarely ever listen to the lyrics. If the song sounds good, I'll listen to it. Obviously "good" is a matter of opinion but the songs I listen to have to be pleasing to the ear so, to me, the lyrics don't matter that much.

- Everyone has had it rough at some point. Some way more than others. Know that nothing that has happened in your past gives you the right to hurt anyone else, aside maybe from the actual perpetrator. There are plenty of successful people in the world who have experienced far greater adversity than you and have overcome that adversity despite their past. You can too. Feeling sorry for ourselves feels good at first until we realize it is not productive and weak. Rise and be strong because once you cross the threshold of committing your own offenses against others, no one will care about your past.

- You may be totally right but, if you come off as a jerk, no one will listen. Relax and present your case, idea, and/or solution in a calm, professional manner and you will be well received, and probably lauded if you're right.

- If your child is sick, try not to become too emotionally distraught so you can focus on their care. Sometimes you must do what is uncomfortable for them (and you, emotionally) to help them. If you coddle them too much it may prolong their recovery. That's not to say that you shouldn't give them plenty of TLC, just do the right thing as well. Make them drink fluids, eat right, get rest, etc. and take solace in the fact that this is helping them grow stronger. I have never experienced a situation where my child has had a serious illness or injury so I don't want to assume I know what people experience in that situation, but I would assume they would have to be even stronger, both emotionally and physically, to do what is necessary to help their child.

- When travelling by plane, if you are sitting on the aisle, there is nothing wrong with standing up and preparing to move once the fasten seat belt light is turned off. You might also help the people in your row by grabbing their bags in order to help expedite everyone leaving the plane.

- The "zipper" method is the most expeditious way to merge traffic from two lanes into one. The problem is there are those who don't believe this and would merge as soon as possible and sit in the right lane for hours instead of using the miles and miles of empty lane to the left to expedite the process. Some who don't believe in the zipper method are not content with doing what they believe is right, some feel the need to hinder others by conducting illegal, dangerous maneuvers like swerving into, or blocking, the empty left lane. Some of the same people who claim to be doing the "right" thing are also the people who have no problem doing the wrong thing. This doesn't make sense to me.

- When it comes to theft, it's not so much that the person is a lazy coward who doesn't want to work for their own stuff but that they are causing a rift in your life. The thieves aren't just taking your things but are inconveniencing you and setting into motion a series of time-consuming events that wouldn't have to be done if the thief hadn't taken your item(s). Events like finding an alternate way to accomplish the task for which the stolen item was used, spending the extra time and money to replace the item, etc. It's a selfish act that proves our society will never be utopian.

- The "cheesy" things are what make your family strong. Don't let anyone deprive you of those bonding times.

- Probably because I've never been in a program, but I don't understand telling people how many days sober you have. It seems like a bleak way to look at it, "I'm 120 days sober, I should relapse any day now" or "120 days closer to death when I won't have to worry about this problem anymore." It's a lot of pressure to constantly remind yourself of your "problem". Let yourself off the hook; free yourself.

It seems like, if you need to count the days/months/years, you haven't changed your way of thinking about the substance because it is still controlling your thoughts. Disregard the substance entirely and move on. Truly, and honestly, leave it behind and become a new you. Instead of keeping track of the time simply change the way you think. Know in your heart and mind that you are not that person anymore and that the substance no longer has power over you. It really is that simple, believe me, I've done it. Continuing to identify as an "addict" or an "alcoholic" sensationalizes what is really happening, you have a control problem. It has little to do with the drug and everything to do with you. Once you make the decision to be a different you then there is no need to label yourself. You are not an addict, or an alcoholic, or anything other than you. Be you, a healthy, responsible, happy, you. Don't rely on a label like you relied on the drug. Having power means not having labels and not cowering to an inanimate object. It means you are free – act accordingly.

- Do we owe those who have wronged us apologies or praise since their actions were a catalyst to our happier future (if applicable)? I am very satisfied and happy with my life, should I be glad of all the adversity I've endured? I say, "I guess?" Yes, I am in a better place, and a better situation, but those people still suck, right? I should be happy with myself for overcoming that adversity, and so should you, if you aren't' already. If you have yet to overcome your adversity, it's never too late. Contact me and let's discuss a way out of your situation: jarrod@tryitlikethis.net

- Why are people so scared of guns, or getting mugged, etc.? Wouldn't it be smarter to overcome these fears by becoming proficient with a firearm, or learn self-defense techniques, etc.? If you're scared of something, educate yourself and train to overcome these fears.

- Cheering at a little league game seems inappropriate. I know it's ok for a child to experience loss, it makes them stronger but, I feel really bad cheering against a little kid, like actually being happy when they make an out if it helps my kid's team? Seems weird.

- When leaders take precautions to prevent catastrophe and that catastrophe doesn't occur, isn't it more appropriate to say "cool, nothing happened" instead of condemning those who made the tough decision? I guarantee that if the situation was reversed and thousands, or millions died everyone would have said the decision makers should have erred on the side of caution. Be wary of those who go against everything their opponent does/says regardless of their opponent's accuracy. These people are not to be trusted.

- All religions probably have the same "god", they just use a different name. There are so many similarities and parallels that it just makes sense that the very first people to refer to a "god" probably broke off from each other and made their own groups with "unique" beliefs. Just look at Christianity, there are several versions of Christianity that have very different rules, I'm sure the same was true when "religions" began.

- School security is not cheating students from being children or from their school experience. There are plenty of schools who have had resource officers, security systems, etc. for decades. These schools are not "prisons", they are a secure place for children to feel safe so they can focus on learning.

- How do people justify blocking a walkway or doorway and carrying on a conversation? Some even give you a look like they're annoyed that you're trying to walk through there. This is another example of people being self-absorbed and not conducive to a utopian society.

- If you're running a meeting your opening better be absolutely hilarious or interesting, otherwise just thank everyone for being there and get down to business. Remember, you're taking up other people's time, probably people who are working for you so don't waste their time with BS.

Meeting Techniques:

o Have an agenda and stick to it.

o State your reason for the meeting and don't let anyone get you off track.

o Always assign a point of contact for each task. If you don't, that task will not be completed.

o Shut down "spotlighters" (people who are just talking to get attention), the true assets to your organization will provide information that is concise, insightful, and valuable.

- Why do people get so butt hurt about poor service? Like they can't believe a human could be horrible. Humans are horrible all the time. Report it and/or drive on.

- If you can prove that you can handle driving at higher speeds, you should be able to. If you are found to be a very nervous driver then you should stay in the right lane. There are people out there driving way faster than they should. I drive at my comfort level and my ability; this should be legal regardless of the speed.

- Stop and smell the roses but don't get in the way of those who don't want to. Some people want to blast through life at 100 miles an hour and no one has the right to hinder them. If someone does hinder someone else, they should accept whatever consequences occur as a result of that hindrance.

- The sitting president should go to the debates of the opposing parties and be allowed to rebut what they say. This would cut down on the BS the other side spews and focus the candidates on the topics at hand. There also needs to be long form debates to truly get to know the candidates.

- This should go without saying but don't break bad on your spouse if you truly love them. Never say anything you'll regret later and always treat them the way you do when you aren't fighting. Too much damage occurs if you go too far and it just chips away at your relationship foundation. If you don't love your spouse, you need to reevaluate what you're doing with your life.

- During the Covid-19 pandemic, people were lauding those who worked "menial" jobs. Were people not already appreciating those who did the "menial" and/or "undesirable" jobs for our society? I had a discussion with some elitists a couple of years ago about this very subject and they said that those people were the dregs and that we shouldn't commend them for aiming too low. I defended these people by saying thank goodness there are people willing, and strong enough, to do these jobs for us.

- "Free" college, isn't. Taxpayers would have to pay for it. Why is there no discussion about the exorbitant amount of money it costs to attend college? Instead of conforming to the "system", why don't we boycott the expensive schools? These universities make billions and still demand unreasonable amounts in tuition. Alas, college is a choice, not a right and colleges are, after all, a business. The better option would be to obtain an affordable degree because most employers couldn't care less where you went to school, only that you did and, actually, more and more don't care if you even went to college.

- Parents: Never take what your children say personally, ever. They don't know what they're saying and forget they've said it shortly after. Blow off the mean, hurtful, awful things they may say and drive on. Most importantly though, under no circumstances, drop down to their level to retaliate. If they cross a line and deserve punishment, ensure you administer it without emotion and speak to them about it afterward.

Chapter 9

Elected Officials and Leaders

Our elected officials are living the good life while their constituents are suffering. Not to get too political but it is appalling that no one acknowledges the fact that most, if not all, of the poverty stricken, feces laden, and generally disregarded districts are run by democrats. It's also amazing that the people in those districts continue to elect these officials who are doing nothing for them. This is not to say that republicans are better but at least they are honest about their goals and plans for the country. Republicans come out and say they are for individual freedom and capitalism, which is a thinly veiled way of saying "handle things on your own" (which most of us would prefer – the less government involvement in my life the better) but it seems democrats tell people what they want to hear regardless of how impossible, and preposterous, it sounds.

If our elected officials, both democrats and republicans,

truly cared about the people they serve, they would be

working tirelessly to improve their respective

districts/states. Unfortunately, our "lawmakers" focus

more on reelection than they ever do on people. Congress

is a money-making scheme first and a "service job" a

distant second, if at all. Actually, their second function is

ensuring their side prevails. This occurs on both sides and

is a waste of taxpayer money. How often do we hear about

a bill that has no chance of passing yet is presented

anyway? This does not serve "we the people" well. The

process should be a formality in that before a bill is

introduced it should already have bi-partisan buy-in.

Representatives and Senators from both sides, and a

presidential rep (if not the President himself, depending on

the gravity of the bill), should sit in a room and figure out

what works best for the people, not just their respective

side, and then finalize the proposed bill and introduce it to

The House as I said, as a formality. Then it should go to the Senate for concurrence (which should be fast since The Senate had a hand in its formulation/finalization), and then off to the White House for approval. This would expedite the process exponentially and actually help the people of this country.

Bills

Speaking of bills presented to Congress, it should be illegal for more than one subject to be included in a bill. Too often unscrupulous Congress members will either try to slip in a "rider" (a provision that has little or nothing to do with the main bill) to try to get the rider approved without anyone knowing or to get the main bill voted down because of the rider attached. A bill should contain one main issue which should be discussed until a workable solution can be achieved. As I mentioned before, representatives from the executive and legislative branches should meet to finalize each bill and stay in that meeting until the work is complete. How many great bills could have been passed if only the proper amount of work had been done? How does the Congress justify including unrelated riders? The answer is they don't have to justify it, the law is written to allow it, and no one is doing anything to prevent it or change the law. The horrible thing is that these people know exactly what they're doing and how despicable it really is. They know that if there is a bill introduced that is very important to the ascension of the country, one that has no chance of being voted down, that a partisan rider has a good chance of being approved. This is a very disgraceful way of doing business but it speaks volumes about the character of the people who utilize this tactic.

People "In Charge"

The problem is that people "in charge" feel like they are most important when the opposite is true. The leaders of our country are responsible for the well-being of the people, not themselves. Rarely do you see any self-sacrifice. Their actions usually seem selfless on the surface, but it usually serves them in some way. It's also disconcerting when people say "we the people" are in charge yet do nothing to ensure that is true. They keep electing the same selfish people to office and continue to suffer. If the people of this country truly wanted change they wouldn't complain that there should be term limits, they would simply vote the current people out of office every 2-3 terms, or sooner if necessary

People in charge (all people in charge, not just elected officials) should feel lucky they are in their positions. When I held leadership positions I always felt humbled by the opportunity and responsibility and tried my hardest to ensure those "under" me had everything they needed. This was especially important in my line because those people were going to war and if they didn't get what they needed it could result in their injury or death. I never respected leaders who walked around like they owned the place and did things simply because they could.

The President

The president is the ultimate public servant. I always found it odd that we treat that position with such reverence when it is a completely elected office that's only prerequisites are that the candidate is a natural born U.S. citizen, has resided in the U.S. for 14 years, and is at least 35 years old. That's it. They are not gods or superheroes, they are simply the person that one of the two major parties decided they wanted as their candidate and then half of the people thought would be a good leader. The president is the least important person in the country, yet we treat him like the most. We guard him as if his absence will somehow result in the country crumbling down. It wouldn't and it won't, we have protocols in place for just such an incident. That's why those in succession for the president are briefed on most, if not all, of what's important (or they should be). The notion that if something happens to the president our nation will weaken is antiquated.

Bureaucracy

People wonder why the government takes so long to accomplish anything, it's called bureaucracy and it is a cancer that no one seems to want to remove. Our leaders are more concerned with how they look and growing their bank account than they do with taking care of the people. I truly believe our Founding Fathers, with all their faults truly cared about the people and the country. The same is not true, and hasn't been for some time, about modern day politicians. They are mostly actors who attempt to replicate politicians' actions before them instead of being themselves. It's painfully obvious how politicians today try so hard to look like politicians instead of simply stating facts, being honest, and actually helping the country. They speak in ambiguities, talking points, and BS. There have been a few lately who have attempted to be genuine but they always fall back into the status quo so their peers take them seriously, as if this is more important that earning the people's respect. When a politician gets behind a microphone they immediately go into fake mode and spew their garbage. But there's a reason why most politicians speak this way, because they are unable to speak any other way and make any sense. Our elected officials are portrayed as if they were anointed sometimes but people fail to realize that politicians are ELECTED, not ordained. They are people, just like us, who convinced their districts to vote for them. Most of the ones I've seen can't even speak with a teleprompter, let alone off the cuff. We need to be more selective in this country or we will continue to get treated the same way we always have. People hate Trump for who he is, how he speaks, and from where he came but the fact that he does what he said he was going to do is indisputable. We just need to find a likeable person who does what's best for the country to unify us. If only all politicians did what they said they would do for us but, they can't because what they promised are lies and impossible to accomplish. The people of this country need to wake up and simply vote people out who have not done what they said they would do. Check their records, hold them accountable.

Frivolous Hearings

How do we let our elected officials get away with holding time, money, and effort wasting investigations and hearings? They have little to no hard evidence, yet they conduct long, drawn out trials that go nowhere or call-in celebrities to testify about nothing and nothing comes of it. I think the elected officials should be fined if it is found that they have been disingenuous when presenting a weak, or non-existent, case for political reasons. It's obvious to everyone but them that their efforts are futile, yet they go forward with the proceedings to showboat and get on TV.

Getting Things Done

Why is it so hard for elected officials to get anything done? For instance, how many times has our own congress been a majority of the same party as the president? Enough to make change, yet they still can't get it done. Why? It's as if they don't want to, maybe to keep the status quo? Maybe they draw things out to give the illusion that they're actually "working"? Maybe they don't care, as long as their investments are doing well (or however else an upper middle-class person reaches millionaire status in a government job). There are a considerable number of problems that seem to have easy fixes or, easy beginnings with a lot of work after yet government works so slow and inefficiently. Issues necessary for the wellbeing of the nation take an exorbitant amount of time to come to fruition, if at all. It's a "secret" society of which only the members really know the rules and goings on. Why don't the so called "crusaders" within the government drop dime on the others? Are they scared? Lack of evidence? Lazy? It's a mystery. There are books documenting what happens when a person is elected to congress and how shady it is, but they don't seem to have made a difference. The only true way to ensure that change occurs is to make it. Voters can impose term limits with their votes but, that would require us all to agree and we know how well that always works. Instead, the same old people keep getting elected and doing nothing besides grandstanding and toeing party lines to make it look like they're doing something so their rich constituents can feel good about themselves. It's amazing how multi-billion-dollar companies can fix problems and grow yet our own government can't figure it out. Perhaps there should be more businessmen and less lawyers in power?

In the military, if you need to rewrite a regulation or standard operating procedure you appoint someone, a point of contact or POC, to either draft one if it doesn't exist or modify the existing one. Then, that POC disseminates the document to those who should have inputs on it along with a "suspense" (time limit for comments/inputs) to get it back to the POC. Once the POC gathers all inputs they incorporate those inputs into the draft for approval by the boss. The boss will make his/her edits and then call a meeting with his/her staff to finalize the document. The document is then signed and everyone is expected to adhere to it. Why can't the government do this? I touched on a bill earlier but, to reiterate, instead of having a bill start in the house (with only a select few people on a committee by the way), and then go to the senate for concurrence, and then to the president for approval, why not get all those entities in the same room (in person or virtually). Once assembled, they can then discuss all the issues that would prevent the bill from becoming law and continue to meet until the bill becomes law. Government officials are our employees, they should answer to us and should be held accountable when they don't perform their job.

Unfortunately, like I said, that would require most of us to agree and that seems like a pipe dream. So, we have the system we have, one that first and foremost benefits those in power and may never benefit all the people it claims to represent. Why don't they follow the same laws as us citizens? It seems like a very simple solution. The problem with this is that it could be easy, but those in power choose to make it hard because they don't have your (the people) best interests at heart.

Picking a candidate

It seems that people gravitate toward a certain type of candidate based on generic views or outlooks on life, but I don't do it that way. I've never had any loyalty to a particular party because both parties are the same and contain the same kinds of people. Now, when I say "party", I'm not talking about all the members but the leadership and candidates. For the most part they are all politicians and only serve themselves. That's what made Trump so different, he couldn't care less about a party, he actually said so on video when he said if he ran for president he would run as a republican because they are easily fooled. I don't think he necessarily "fooled" everyone, he was simply the last candidate left standing, mainly because the other candidates were weak and couldn't stand toe to toe with him. If there was a strong candidate who made sense and could trade jabs with Trump, he probably would have won the nomination and possibly the presidency. Unfortunately, the people who could challenge Trump don't run for office.

As I said, I don't have any loyalty to any party, I look at the candidate as a person and evaluate their positions on issues that affect this country. This seems like the most logical conclusion but our country doesn't work that way. Most people either vote all republican or all democrat because it's easier. Some are under the impression that their party's candidates have their best interest in mind, or they stand to benefit from their party's candidates getting elected. Elections really have very little to do with the individual (as illustrated with the left's support of Biden). Yes, some candidates appear to care and appear to be "different", but they quickly conform to the system, mainly out of survival, but also because they, deep down, are politicians and that's what politicians do, take care of themselves first. I don't think we need anymore "career politicians" in our government. I think we need people who are smart in the ways of government but are true public servants who are focused on the job of actually helping people instead of making themselves rich. It can't be an issue of compensation since most politicians gain wealth in office. It probably has more to do with the hassle of running for office and the scrutiny that befalls candidates.

Most people who would do a great job serving others don't want their lives upended. Politicians seem to welcome it or at least not mind it. It should be illegal to "expose" a candidate when you don't have clear cut evidence of the accusation against a person. Just mentioning something that MAY have happened in the candidate's past can ruin them. Once it's out there people immediately believe it and by the time the actual truth comes out the candidate has endured massive amounts of accusations and detestation that it's almost impossible to bounce back. The story should be airtight before it can surface and, if the story is disproven then the originators, and all who proliferated the lie, should be held accountable.

Abolish Political Parties

There shouldn't be parties, they should be outlawed because they limit the choices during an election. How can two non-governmental organizations have so much power over our government? How did we let this happen? How do we as a society let these two corrupt organizations manipulate us by only allowing us to choose between two people?

We don't actually have to let them choose for us. There are laws and stipulations that allow for others to be on the ballot, but we fear the "third party" vote because we feel it's a vote for the other side. This is lunacy, especially for the party who obviously has a weak candidate. Why do they let their "party" decide for them? The craziest example is happening as I write this, 77-year-old Joe Biden is the democrat presidential candidate. The party that is supposed to be representing anyone other than old, straight, white males has an old, straight, white male as their candidate. They had homosexuals, women, and dark-skinned people vying for the presidency and they disregarded all of them to select the guy who looks most like their idea of their opponent. It really makes you wonder what exactly is going on with the presidential election. How does Joe Biden represent the democrat base?

It's crazy. Yet, he's the candidate and now everyone on the left has to back him. Like I said, they don't have to, they can start a grassroots campaign for someone else and simply write that person in. But this will never happen because that would entail people coming together and, again, we know how that usually works out.

Campaign Finance

There should be a cap on campaign finance as well. Each candidate should have a cap on how much they can raise and how much they can spend. This would level the playing field and allow those who don't have much money to stay in the race. The amount of money raised usually has very little to do with how good the candidate is. People who can buy the most ad time, etc. shouldn't be the only choices for us.

Speaking of campaign finance reform, my daughter had a good idea: when raising campaign finances, make it mandatory that a portion must be used to help the country in some way. Force the candidates to put their money where their mouth is by choosing a program that helps the people the candidate means to lead. In that same vein, my daughter asked why the government can't simply ask for money from our wealthier citizens, the "1%". It's not a bad idea, simply present a program that helps U.S. citizens and ask wealthy citizens and corporations to fund, and run, it. The private sector has long proven its ability to successfully manage programs the government consistently fails to. I realize this last part has nothing to do with campaign finance but maybe limiting funds from wealthy donors will focus their efforts on more philanthropic issues?

Chapter 10

Presidential Goals

I've heard people say something to the effect that those who seek the presidency are "insane" and, judging from some of the candidates we've seen in recent years, they're partially correct. I say partially because, for a servant of the people, the presidency is, or should be, the pinnacle of service. It's amazing how the presidency has become a job where only the richest and most popular people are elected. "Shouldn't the most popular person be elected?" you ask. Yes, but popular for the right reasons. They should be elected for their actions that illustrate their desire to not only lead but, more importantly, to serve.

Service

Speaking of service, my entire life has been about service. From a career in the military to working for child protection in Alaska to working as a contractor for the U.S. Government, all my jobs have been in the service of others. Include my work as a Girl Scout Leader, swim and soccer coach, youth group leader, and school chaperone and you can see that serving others has been a large part of my life. Most of the time I was either in a position to help and did so or was specifically asked and I accepted. I think more things would get done if more people did the same thing. Being presented with an opportunity, or specifically asked to help, is much easier than seeking out volunteer or service opportunities. If more people took advantage of these situations, I believe our world would be better for everyone.

As you can see, I'm not a politician, I'm a servant of the people and through that lens, as President, I'll view all the issues that come across my desk. The presidency, and any other elected position, should be so absolutely exhausting that incumbents wouldn't want another term. They should be so spent from serving the people who elected them that they have no other choice but to not seek reelection.

Objectives

1. Due to the Covid-19 outbreak, we have proven that the government can conduct business remotely or not at all. Think how much money this can save. This pandemic has proven just how insignificant most government agencies are. There are those who are not benefitting from teleworking or unable to and they should certainly be able to work with precautions in place. Hopefully by the time you read this we have a vaccine, but we have proven that the government can operate in this situation with considerably less people going into work.

2. I don't think there should be a tax on winning.

   Whether it be at the casino, lottery, a

   game show, etc. Why should you have to pay the

   government for something you won?

   It makes no sense. I do, however, think there

   should be an exorbitant tax on "decision"

   items, things you make a choice to purchase, but

   don't necessarily need. Things that

   don't really serve any other purpose other than to

   "entertain". Food, clothing, shelter

   (primary shelter, not a summer home) shouldn't be

   taxed at all. We need these items to

   survive, why are we penalized for buying them? If

   someone chooses to buy something

   they don't "need" (based on the bottom three levels

   of Maslow's Hierarchy of Needs)

   then they should pay tax on it.

3. Another way we can save this country money is to go to a four day/thirty-two-hour work week. If not for everyone then just government agencies. Believe me, government employees waste a lot of time at work. Why not give them more time with their families and decrease their stress levels? Not only that but stagger the times people come in and leave each day. It's ludicrous that we make every single government employee come in at the same time, causing traffic jams, etc. Then they all take lunch at the same time, resulting in more traffic and huge lines at the same restaurants everyone uses due to their distance from work. Then we make them all leave at the same time creating an even bigger traffic jam. People spend way too much time in their cars getting from home to work and back again. This is lunacy that can be stopped. There is no need, as proven with all the Covid-19 teleworking, to have everyone in person, at their desk, at the same time. If

you need someone, call them. If there is a meeting, telecom. If someone must sign something, have them sign it electronically. There will be times when everyone is at work at the same time and can have the "vital" in person meeting, but we all know what a waste of time most meetings are so why not just send an email or conduct a video teleconference? If it requires discussion, telecom. If only some of the people are there, have them meet and the rest telecom. For most people, a secure telecom is only necessary occasionally. When it is, make sure everyone knows and they can all show up in person. Some will scoff at this proposition but only because they can't envision it. They have been stuck in this 40 hour/5-day work week rut for so long that they can't imagine anything else. I can't believe people haven't demanded more time off. We go in on Monday and "work" for 5 days and then get two days off? It's not even two days really. On Sunday you must mentally prepare for Monday, so you really only have Saturday to yourself. We spend most of our lives at work and most people probably aren't working a full 40 hours anyway. Why not give them an extra day so they're not burnt out by Friday? There are those who love to be at work and to them I say "great! Work from home or go into work and "get some stuff done" but I don't think it's necessary. Government "production" can't get any worse so why not give people an extra day to live their lives? I know what the government will say: "we're paying you to be here, so you need to be here" which is the craziest thing I've ever heard. They're paying people to be in a building, at a desk, in the hopes that they'll be productive but, from what I've experienced, that seldom happens.

Some might say that people rely on government agencies to be there for them and to that

I say, hire more workers and instill split schedules. Some people could work Monday through Thursday while others work Tuesday through Friday. Another way to alleviate this issue is to move everything online. Forego the necessity to speak to someone or visit an actual office. Take Estonia, for instance. The only thing you can't do online in Estonia is get married, divorced, and conduct real estate transactions. Everything else is done online. This would allow most government workers to assist customers from anywhere (if necessary), allow people 24/7 access to their information, and significantly decrease operating costs.

4. Speaking of "government", I've been using that word like it's an entity in and of itself, but the government is made of many different people, who all have differing views of how employees should behave. Some couldn't care less about the clock;

others care too much and watch the clock like the government is going to shut down if a person is 5 minutes late. Then there are those who lead their people in a way that empowers them and enables them to be self-starters (and finishers) ensuring that they feel valued which leads to them wanting to be there and wanting to work. When I was in the military, and lead troops, I couldn't have cared less what time they got to work or what time they left as long as things got done. If it took them shorter than the "duty day" to get the work done, they would cut out early and if the job required more of the "duty day" they would stay longer. Our government has never, really, been "results" driven, only time driven, which is odd given that an entity is successful based on their accomplishments, not their time in the building. I've seen some government employees do absolutely nothing all day long yet brag about how they were in before everyone and left after everyone.

"I put in my time" they'd say but had nothing to show for it and contributed zilch to the progress of the country. Very weird thing to brag about, being on time, when that's not the goal. Now, if there is a meeting where people are waiting on you, show up on time. If you must do something at a specific time, be there 15 minutes early. But if your job is results oriented, not time oriented, why is it important when you get there and when you leave? I've had jobs where I was the last one in and the first one out and I did PT while I was there and took a lunch break and still did exponentially more than most of the people in the office. It's about results and actual work. Which is why a 32 hour/4-day work week is a good idea, it gives people more of a break so they might be more productive when they are at work, not to mention it saves on electricity, water, etc.

5. We also need more Federal holidays. At least on per month on a Thursday with a "family" day on the following Monday and, since we are now operating under a 4 day/32-hour work week, it will result in a five-day weekend each month. Most people are wasting their lives at work and I believe that they would be more productive if they received more time off.

6. I would give federal grants for school security, to include, but not limited to, resource officers, security systems, and metal detectors. It'll be part of the education budget and be mandatory. You want to prevent school shootings, defend against them.

7. I would provide funding to law enforcement agencies but, in order to get the money, they must pass physical fitness, mobility (tactical driving, accident avoidance, etc.), medical, and marksmanship tests. If

a department doesn't have enough officers to allow for them to train on these tasks during work hours, then the numbers of officers must be increased. This may seem unrealistic but not compared to the billions of dollars wasted on programs that do not benefit the nation. The funding will be used to hire more officers to allow for training during work hours and to hire experts to train officers on the aforementioned tasks. Another option is to form a federal agency that trains police departments across the U.S. This agency would be comprised of experts in the skills mentioned above. In addition to these tasks, LEOs would be given periodic psych evaluations and receive monthly, if not weekly, training in negotiation techniques. Every LEO should be an expert in the four basic tasks but also have the mental training to only need those skills once negotiations have failed.

Government Social Programs

There has been much controversy and discussion about the implications of allowing people to procreate at will. On the one hand, people are free to have as many children as they want but they are also responsible for those children. However, in this country, we incentivize having children, an unfortunate byproduct of helping people. The government saw that people, mostly single mothers, were struggling to take care of their children so they reached out to help but, in doing so, they made it very lucrative to keep having children – the very definition of a vicious cycle. Objectives continued:

8. There should be a cap on how many children a family can claim to receive government funds. If you continue to have children knowing that you

cannot support them then you are being

irresponsible and should not be rewarded for such

behavior. There must be stipulations for people

who receive "government help" (which is just

another way of saying "taxpayer money"). It is

unfair for those who pay taxes and do not receive

government help to pay for those who are

irresponsible and live outside their means. I realize

that there are circumstances outside a person's

control like a breadwinning spouse leaving or

dying, etc. but I don't believe this is always the case

and each case should be evaluated to ensure the

legitimacy of the claim. Also, once the legitimacy

of the claim is established, there needs to be a plan

implemented to wean the recipient off government

assistance so they can operate on their own. There

must also be drug testing and frequent visits to

check receipts to ensure the money is being spent

appropriately. The idea of simply giving out money

to people who have already been irresponsible or are "gaming" the system is ludicrous. Again, I realize that not everyone is doing this but, unfortunately those who are make it hard for everyone. The government, in order to be good stewards of the people's money, must scrutinize every beneficiary to ensure they are not trying to defraud the government and steal taxpayer money.

9. This model also applies to those who seek health care from the government. People are demanding free universal health care paid for by those who pay for their own health care and pay taxes that would cover this "free" health care for all. Usually those who demand free health care don't pay taxes at all anyway so it's a "win" for them. I'm not against helping people with their health care and, while it shouldn't be "free", it should be attainable. If the government was in the health care business for all

people, there should be stipulations like the beneficiary must exercise, and eat correctly, not smoke or do drugs, etc. This would lower the chances of people needing health care and keep the cost low. If we simply gave out free healthcare but didn't insist on people living healthy lifestyles, the program would be unsustainable (not that it wouldn't be anyway given the government's track record on running things.) Again, if you are requesting assistance from an entity, whomever they are, it is not unreasonable to follow their rules to receive that assistance. If people feel these stipulations are unfair then they should provide for themselves and free themselves of any outside control.

State's Rights and Responsibilities

U.S. States should have the freedom to govern themselves if the laws do not affect other states, and for the most part they do. Each state in the union is so unique it is impossible to have a "one size fits all" model for all states. The federal government should be limited to border security, foreign affairs, interstate travel and commerce, etc. The federal government should only be involved if the issue affects all states equally. I think the federal government has far too much overreach and doesn't allow the states to freely operate how they want. I also think that we should reform the financial aid each state receives from the federal government. The focus of the federal government should be balancing the budget, getting rid of the debt, and rebuilding/improving infrastructure. This country was founded on hard work and dedication, our leaders should have that same focus. I believe the states should be allowed to thrive or fail as they deserve. If the governments of failing states aren't doing their job correctly then the people need to vote them out of office. It is not the federal government's job to bail out those who choose not to help themselves. People need to stop feeling helpless against their government and start taking a proactive position against those who do not act accordingly. It only takes a short internet search to find out your elected official's voting record and, if they are not voting correctly according to what your state wants, then vote them out of office, the same should be done for state legislatures. The people hold the true power, but they simply won't wield it. They vote with fear, or tradition, or based on lies they've been told. We need to come together as one community, set our differences aside, and control the government with our votes to prevent the government from controlling us.

Federal Budget

We need to hold our government accountable for not balancing the budget. It's unacceptable for us to expect people to pay their taxes, etc. when the government can't even "live" within their means. A complete review and revamping of the federal budget must be accomplished. The COVID-19 pandemic illustrated just how much money we waste and how few agencies/employees we need to operate the country. The problem is that the proper time and effort is not being applied to this endeavor therefore it will always be an issue. The government needs to revisit all outgoing payments to determine their validity. If it does not directly contribute to the betterment of the U.S. and its citizens, it should be stopped. The government is not a good steward of the people's money, as illustrated by all the frivolous senate hearings and congressional inquiries that occur.

Our country also needs to find more revenue streams. We need to collect on debts owed to us, and we could also do things like hold a nationwide lottery or legalize gambling in all states. Whatever we decide it must be implemented because taxing our people to cover everything doesn't seem to be working. Currently, we only receive 5% of our income from "other" sources. The rest is in some form of tax and most of it is income tax, a tax that 44% of the people in the nation don't pay. This is unacceptable. Everyone should pay something. If this occurred then everyone, theoretically, could pay less. The only "fair" way to tax people is to make everyone pay the same percentage. This seems very simple and effective, but I don't think the government is concerned with simplicity and they obviously aren't concerned at all with effectiveness. If our elected officials were as concerned with improving this country as they were with getting reelected, we would be in much better shape. The amount of money that is wasted by our government each year is unimaginable, think about how many people could be helped if the budget was scrutinized and fixed. But our government has proven time and again that they are not interested in the people of this country but only staying in power.

Federal Transparency

Also, there needs to be significantly more transparency. Classified briefings aside, each decision-making process should be recorded and archived for the American people to see. Before a decision is made the American people must be allowed to review the process. If our decision makers knew that every word was being scrutinized they would choose them wisely. There should also be a video made to explain each initiative in layman's terms to ensure Americans know what is happening. Each discussion needs to include subject matter experts to ensure our leaders are making the correct decisions because being elected to an office, in no way, qualifies you to make decisions or magically makes you an expert. It really is amazing that we hold our elected officials in such high regard when the only thing they did was get more votes than the other candidate.

Government is also an inherent naysayer. People who work for the government are trained to say "no". No to new initiatives, no to spending more on valid programs, no to increased efficiency, no to cutting budgets of unnecessary programs, etc.

Education

As I state elsewhere in this book, the U.S. education system is broken, and no one is interested in fixing it. Mainly because it seems impossible but, we need to revamp the education system to instill a love of learning instead of a fear of testing. The idea of "grades" and traditional "progression" is antiquated. Children need to learn, not have anxiety about passing tests. They need to be excited about the subjects. There should definitely be evaluations to check the progress of the students, but it should be as they go, not a cumulative exam after everything has been taught. This is just one option, I'm sure there are others, but the main focus should be ensuring children are educated properly before moving to the next level. Unfortunately, as I stated, no one is interested in the individual student. They simply want to push kids through knowing that not every kid will be set up for success after they graduate.

The Department of Education needs to either be reorganized, downsized, or disbanded. Either that or they need to recruit its members from the "front lines" of education (teachers). There should be Federal Representatives from each state that are immersed in the educational process of their state to ensure the Federal level is properly informed. If you solicit help from anyone else you run the risk of hiring a "spotlighter" or someone who is only interested in getting recognition instead of actually helping. It's sad how most administrators think they have to change something or spend money to be successful when all they really need to do is listen to their schools and help them achieve their goals. Instead, you get self-serving "woke" "intellectuals' who think they know better than everyone else. It really is sad to see so much time, money, and effort wasted on frivolous programs that don't actually benefit the students.

Another issue with the education system in this country is that the school "year" is not conducive to working parents. There are too many days off and the children should go to school through the summer. This would decrease summer learning loss and solve the childcare issue for families during the summer break.

Early outs are also a significant hindrance to working families, single parents, etc. They disrupt the tight, and fragile, schedule most families use to make everything work. How does the school district, state, federal government justify making families adjust their schedule periodically so the school can have a teacher's workshop, etc. What is a family supposed to do when their child usually gets out of school at 3:30 but, on occasion, they get out at 1:30 or 2:00? Now the parents must either get off work early, and possibly lose leave/sick days, or lose pay. This is what I mean when I say the Administrators don't have the best interests of the children in mind when they make their decisions.

Voting

We seriously can't figure out how to streamline voting? Everyone has a social security number. One SSN, one vote, period. This ensures that only U.S. citizens vote. Why can't we vote online? Corporations have state of the art computer systems that safeguard your information. The Federal Government should be able to create a computer system, or use existing technology, where everyone can vote online using their SSN. Or we could shift the election cycle to line up with tax season. When you file your tax return you also vote. If you don't file a return, you don't vote.

Pharmaceutical Issues

We need to figure out a way for people to obtain affordable prescription drugs while continuing to encourage drug innovation. I think both are equally important but there are those who feel that, if we don't allow drug companies to overcharge for their products then they will stop innovating thereby reducing the amount of effective prescription drugs. There are many ways to remedy this issue but the one that comes to mind is to rearrange the federal budget to free up money to assist these companies. Another solution is to ask the best pharmaceutical scientists to work for the government as private contractors or DOD civilians. The pay would still be commensurate with their abilities/work, but we could ensure the cost to the consumer remains low. This would also allow us to let other companies manufacture the same drugs to drive prices down. As it stands, the prescription drugs are patented which prevents anyone else from manufacturing them thereby driving up the cost. Another factor that prevents us from controlling how prescription drugs are made and distributed is that China controls much of our prescription drug trade, among many other things.

There are also plenty of generic drugs that are generic, but they are often overlooked to make more money for the pharmaceutical companies. Also, we are now finding that generic drugs are being made by unscrupulous companies that lie about how their drugs are made and thereby disseminating substandard drugs. If the U.S. took over generic drug manufacturing and distribution, we could ensure they were made correctly and sold cheaply. This could be paid for by the profits from the drugs, costing the taxpayer nothing. However, a lot of these drugs would become unnecessary if we focused more on physical fitness and eating correctly.

China

How have we allowed China to control so much of our country? Well, because it makes good business sense. Our government has made it so difficult and expensive to manufacture items here that most companies have resorted to overseas production. Look at any product and more often than not it was made in China. The little "Made in China" stickers are everywhere. How could this have happened? How does a superpower, a superpower that used to be number one, allow another superpower to undermine them as much as China has us and still allow China to be so vital to our economic survival? Fair trade and diplomacy are absolutely necessary, but we also need to ensure we're not being taken advantage of.

Immigration

I believe we should allow any immigrant who wants to work in our country to obtain a work visa and come into this country. We need good, hard working immigrants in the U.S., but we also need to ensure they contribute to the country by paying a portion of what they make to the government. This sounds like paying taxes but it's more like a fee to come here and work. They should not be allowed to vote until they become citizens, but they should be allowed to take advantage of some of the benefits of living in the U.S. If they want to work here they should be fingerprinted, photographed, investigated, and provided an identification card. They must also have a plan before they enter the U.S. This information should be kept in a database to ensure we know who exactly is in this country. If there are those who come here and do not obtain the proper credentials then they should be assessed to see if they are an asset to the U.S. and, if they are not, they should be deported to their home country. I doubt there will be many immigrants who fall into the latter category but, if they do, then they are probably here for unscrupulous reasons and need to leave anyway. A large problem is the lack of ICE and/or border patrol agents. We need to allot more funding to not only our border security and enforcement but border operations as well. I'm the last person to get upset about the way we treat those who enter the country illegally because those people chose to come here but, the way we run our border detention centers seems inefficient and must be overhauled/streamlined. This takes money and resources. People complain about the treatment of illegals, yet they don't want to spend money to properly handle the situation. The bottom line though is that we can't allow illegal immigration because bad people come across too. It's the job of the federal government to ensure the safety of its citizens and letting anyone in without documenting them first is failing at that job. We need to streamline the path to citizenship, simplify it, and increase the number of people working on approving citizenships. Increase the number of people working immigration issues. U.S. citizens complain so much about illegal immigration, yet no one does anything substantial about it.

We also need to work better with Mexico to solve the immigration issue. It should be a joint effort to ensure the safety of both our country's citizens. There should be more official border crossing points with both countries occupying a station on their respective side of the border. We should solicit help from Mexico to discourage illegal border crossings and encourage legal ones. Mexico should prepare its citizens for crossing our border so when they get to our side, they need only be printed and photographed for our database before they can be sent on their way.

Issues to pursue after more fact-finding missions:

Issue 1: Space

At the time of this writing, the private sector has partnered with the U.S. Government to restart the space program. This is long overdue. Yes, there is an argument to keep humans on one planet, so we don't pollute another one but, I don't think that concern outweighs the need to explore. Pushing farther out into space allows us to explore more of it. Why wouldn't we want to invest in creating new technologies that may someday allow us to explore the outer reaches of our solar system, and beyond? Also, it would be amazing to make space travel available to all. Seems extraneous and unnecessary but, life is about living and doing as many amazing things as you can, why wouldn't we try? Especially given the increased interest by the private sector. Having private corporations involved with space travel, like everything else, will increase the efficiency and probably produce a far superior product.

Issue 2: Farming

There is a growing problem in this country regarding the availability, and quality, of food. While industrial farming has provided many advantages, it doesn't seem to be enough. There are also concerns about overuse of chemicals, etc. Perhaps it's time to focus on not only industrial farming but sustainable farming as well. If we continue to abuse the land for the current generation there might not be land available for future generations. I believe it's important to focus on both equally. Those who are here now must be cared for but, it can't be at the cost of our children, grandchildren, etc. We must insist that agriculture be productive and beneficial to the world while not destroying the land on which it uses to grow. Some think that, if we continue to conduct industrialized farming that the land will become unusable in the very near future thereby leaving us with no means to grow food.

Issue 3: Guns

Guns are a divisive subject in this country and I'm not sure why. The 2nd Amendment clearly states that *"the right of the people to keep and bear Arms, shall not be infringed"*. This doesn't mean that you can bear arms sometimes or only in certain places, this means it's your right to bear arms. There are those who post signs in certain places stating that bearing arms is prohibited. By whose authority? The constitution allows us to bear arms and I believe it takes more than a sign to change that. Having signs such as these begs the question: Why? Why are they prohibiting a person's right to bear arms in that location/situation? Are they fearful that someone will use it? Are they fearful that a crime may be committed by the person bearing arms? A sign will not stop a criminal from committing crime, if that were true all shop owners should put up "robbing prohibited" signs instead. The fact is that when you put up a sign attempting to violate a citizen's 2nd Amendment rights you put them in danger and make them vulnerable to those who would not abide by a sign. It's odd that this needs to be explained.

Issue 4: Incentivizing Charity

There is a lot of charity work being done but it doesn't seem to be enough. We need to make it lucrative for people to be charitable. There may already be programs in place, but they clearly aren't doing enough. There needs to be an aggressive effort to ensure a corporation, before they can operate in an area, has done something to help the less fortunate in the community. Some examples: The Starbucks Community Center, The Tesla Sports Complex, The Amazon Homeless Shelter, or the Disney Foster Home. These corporations make billions, why not ask them to help those less fortunate?

Yes, I believe we should invest in foster homes. There are too few foster families for the number of foster children in this country. If we make a state-of-the-art foster home with all the amenities a child needs, we can make it a positive experience and help these kids who normally wouldn't have an advantage over those in a family setting. The facilities could have classes on finance, fitness, and other life lessons. They could have tutors on staff to assist with homework. Comfortable facilities that make a child feel welcome and comfortable and a staff that has been vetted and cleared to ensure those caring for foster children are doing it for the right reasons and not just to get a paycheck. These facilities need a staff that truly cares for the children and has their best interest at heart. Most importantly, the staff must have the ability to put the child's needs above their own, at least while they're at work.

Issues that need work:

1. Hungry American Children – figure out a way to tap into the 150,000 tons of food wasted each day and disseminate it to, at least, hungry children.

2. Educational Inequality – subsidies for those less fortunate communities.

3. Vertical Farms – dig deeper to determine its worth.

4. Homelessness – get them off the street and into a bed.

5. China, Russia, Iran, North Korea – work to mitigate tensions, increase good will, and prevent conflict.

6. Child Protection Agencies – should be standardized across the U.S. to streamline procedures, interstate transfers, etc.

7. Military Spending – must be scrutinized. There is a lot of waste that still occurs, and it is not with the lower units. The massive waste is usually at the highest levels of the military yet lower levels are always forced to suffer first. This results in lack of training, equipment and overall preparedness for

combat. Also, a look at the Defense Commissary Agency must be taken to ensure it is performing as necessary.

Epilogue

If you are wondering why I care so much about what other people do, especially given that I specifically said not to in this book, it's because I care about helping people and getting to the root of the problem is the best way to do this. The point of this life is to be an individual, not caring so much about fitting and accepting others for being individuals. The more individuals we have the less mob mentality and less craziness. Be wary of anyone who seeks power, "likes", or recognition for they do not have your best interests in mind.

Email questions to: jarrod@tryitlikethis.net. Keep them as short and to the point as possible while still giving pertinent details and I will do my best to help. Also, try to keep as much emotion out of the question as possible, emotions may feel right but are a hindrance to solutions.

You may not do everything you want in life, but do everything you can.

About the Author

Jarrod Welsh

Jarrod Welsh retired from the US Air Force after ~24 years of service, over half being with special operations. Following his retirement he worked in Child Protection for two years and is currently a military contractor. He and his wife also write children's books and have four children.

Twitter: @TryItLikeThis
IG: @jarrod_TryItLikeThis
FB: @TryItLikeThis
Web: tryitlikethis.net

__Notes__

Notes

Made in the USA
Middletown, DE
26 September 2021